A JOURNEY TO THE HEART OF JESUS

Guideposts Along the Way

J. PETER SARTAIN

Our Sunday Visitor Publishing Division
Our Sunday Visitor, Inc.
Huntington, Indiana 46750

19 18 17 16 15 14 1 2 3 4 5 6 7 8 9

ISBN: 978-1-61278-768-8 (Inventory No. T1574)
eISBN: 978-1-61278-351-2
LCCN: 2013950317

Cover design: Lindsey Riesen
Cover photo: Shutterstock
Interior design: Dianne Nelson
Interior photo: Photo on page 42 courtesy of the author.

PRINTED IN THE UNITED STATES OF AMERICA

Of you my heart speaks; you my glance seeks;
Your presence, O Lord, I seek.
Psalm 27:8

Table of Contents

ACKNOWLEDGMENTS

Most of the Scripture texts in this work are taken from the *New American Bible, revised edition*, © 2010, 1991, 1986, 1970, Confraternity of Christian Doctrine, Washington, D.C., and are used by permission of the copyright owner. All rights reserved. No part of the *New American Bible* may be reproduced in any form without permission in writing from the copyright owner.

The texts of Psalm 22:10, 20, 23, 25, 31 and Psalm 27:8 are from the *Lectionary for Mass for Use in the Dioceses of the United States of America*, second typical edition, © 2001, 1998, 1997, 1986, 1970, Confraternity of Christian Doctrine, Inc., Washington, D.C. Used with permission. All rights reserved.

Excerpts from Night Prayer for Monday, the Office of Readings for July 11 and Tuesday of the Thirty-Fourth Week in Ordinary Time, 1 Kings 8:51-53, and Exodus 19:4 are from the *Liturgy of the Hours*, © 1970, 1973, 1975, International Committee on English in the Liturgy Corporation (ICEL). All rights reserved.

Excerpts from Preface I of Saints and Preface of All Saints are from *The Roman Missal*, © 2010, International Committee on English in the Liturgy Corporation (ICEL). All rights reserved.

Excerpts from St. John Paul II's Angelus address (June 11, 1989), apostolic letter *Novo Millennio Ineunte* ("At the Beginning of the New Millennium"), and Pope Benedict XVI's encyclical *Spe Salvi* ("Saved in Hope"), © 2014, Libreria Editrice Vaticana.

English translation of the *Catechism of the Catholic Church* for the United States of America, © 1994, United States Catholic Conference, Inc. — Libreria Editrice Vaticana. English translation of the *Catechism of the Catholic Church: Modifications from the Editio Typica*, © 1997, United States Catholic Conference, Inc. — Libreria Editrice Vaticana.

INTRODUCTION

Chief among a bishop's roles is that of teacher. We teach through homilies, through lectures, perhaps in a classroom, during retreats, and most of all, we hope, through example. Many of us also make use of diocesan publications to speak to our parishioners through regular columns, as I have done since becoming a bishop in 2000.

This book is a collection of columns I have written for the official publications of the Diocese of Little Rock (*Arkansas Catholic*), the Diocese of Joliet (*Catholic Explorer* and *Christ Is Our Hope*), and the Archdiocese of Seattle (*The Catholic Northwest Progress* and *Northwest Catholic*). It follows another collection of columns, *Of You My Heart Has Spoken*, published in 2005.

These are simple words, intended to convey a message of hope in Jesus Christ. Originally written for the most part as stand-alone pieces, they have been arranged in this book according to seven broad themes. Perhaps you will find a thought here or there which will strike at your heart as an invitation to accept God's surpassing love for you poured out in his Son, Jesus, and nurtured in the Church. Nothing would please me more.

I owe a debt of gratitude to the editors and staff of the publications mentioned above. Without exception, they encouraged and helped me take on this regular opportunity to teach through writing. I thank my sister, Sister Marian, O.P., who patiently edited these columns for publication as a book and suggested the arrangement you find here, as well as titles for individual pieces. I thank my good friend Sister Rose Marie Dillman, S.P., for proofreading the printed text. I thank the staff of the Office of Communications of the Archdiocese of Seattle, especially Greg Magnoni, Kevin Birnbaum, and Ellen Bollard, for their invaluable assistance in the preparation of the book.

As disciples of Christ, we are all on pilgrimage. May our journey lead us to the Heart of Jesus. And may the selections in this book serve as guideposts along the way.

✠ J. PETER SARTAIN
Archbishop of Seattle

CHAPTER 1
DISCIPLESHIP IS A PILGRIMAGE

A Pilgrimage, Not a Freeway

On moving to Illinois in 2006, I underwent the normal newcomer rituals: I took the written driver's test, received an Illinois driver's license, registered to vote, opened a local bank account, and perhaps most significantly of all, acquired an I-Pass. Not having regularly driven on toll roads in Arkansas or Tennessee, I found the I-Pass automatic credit card deductions an altogether new experience. No doubt in my pre-I-Pass weeks I paid tolls when I did not need to, failed to pay when I should have, and sped through the I-Pass lane oblivious to the fact that I now owed money to the state of Illinois.

But after a few months, I was driving almost like a freeway veteran. Almost.

I understood the toll-road system, more or less, but there were two things that still left me rattled: the brazen speeding of many drivers and their impatience with newcomers like me who didn't yet know which exit to take toward our destination. Everyone but me seemed to know that the speed limit is actually eighty, and everyone but me seemed to know precisely where they were going. The rush, the speed, and the impatience gave new meaning to "peer pressure."

Since moving to Washington State in 2010, I've had similar experiences of initiation. I have traded in my I-Pass for a Good-to-Go Pass, but the rest is, as Yogi Berra famously said, "déjà vu all over again." Cars and trucks roam the freeways in intimidating packs, and the pressure to join the passing throng is considerable. My reluctance to change lanes quickly in heavy traffic has caused me to miss my exit a few times and has probably irritated other drivers.

Every day, every trip, and every task can become a pilgrimage if we decide to live that way.

It's not the possibility of getting lost that intimidates but the unrelenting speed, the pressure, the feeling that I must do what everyone else is doing — and do it quickly.

Since I spend a great deal of time on the freeways, I have reflected on the experience often and think it helps illustrate a simple but important aspect of the Christian life — that we follow a different way.

The pressure is great to follow unquestioningly the prevailing trends. The temptation is formidable to consider those trends acceptable precisely because everyone seems to be following them. Speed is spectacularly alluring because it has an air of efficiency, confidence, and exhilaration. But speed also carries spectacular hazards, especially the hazards of superficiality and indifference.

Modern life is much like a freeway. But discipleship is a pilgrimage.

A pilgrimage is not quickly accomplished, and it entails frequent stops along the way for observing, pondering, praying, and resting with loved ones and with God. A pilgrimage can take place in a big city in the clamor of rush hour, as packs of cars speed by, horns honking impatiently. Every day, every trip, and every task can become a pilgrimage if we decide to live that way.

A pilgrimage is a deliberate journey, and to make a pilgrimage one must first slow down — even if everyone else is speeding.

Those making a pilgrimage never pass others along the way without looking them warmly in the eye and recognizing in them a sister or a brother — even if they nervously avert their eyes when we do.

Those making a pilgrimage recognize that each day offers the opportunity to learn a new lesson, deepen a relationship, and mend a fence.

Those making a pilgrimage punctuate the day with peace: a few deep breaths when tensions flare, a few moments of deliberate silence, or a few kind words with colleagues sharpen the focus and lighten the load.

Those making a pilgrimage carry joy, not tension, from place to place. When they walk through the door, everyone's spirits are lifted.

Those making a pilgrimage stop regularly to pray. Pray for the person who looked away. Pray for those rushing by, faces lined with worry. Pray to be better persons. Pray to grow closer to God. Pray to be instruments of peace. Pray for no reason at all.

Those making a pilgrimage reflect on God's word as life's roadmap — a lamp for the feet, as the psalmist says.

Those making a pilgrimage take God's hand and let him lead, even through the dark valley, when the pavement runs out.

Those making a pilgrimage have a destination — to be with God forever — but know that even though the journey may not end today, whatever happens today is an important step in that direction. For them no day is ever unimportant, no step — however halting or small — is without possibilities.

Those making a pilgrimage do not rush through life. They hope through life. They recognize that just as each day is a gift from God, so can each day be returned to God as a gift, a gift he will accept with love.

A Methodist minister friend once told me a beautiful story about pilgrimages. It seems that a missionary to Native Americans was collecting money from church members for a new building. A frail, elderly woman who lived many miles from church walked the long distance to contribute her widow's mite. The minister thanked her for her generosity but added, "You did not have to walk all this way. I would have gladly come to you." Surprised, she responded, "My journey was part of the gift."

So it is with us. Even if the world rushes around us, we can give each moment to God. We are on a pilgrimage, not a freeway.

Christ Is the *Way* and Destination

My seminary rector was fond of saying, "If you don't know where you're going, any road will get you there." Although we frequently quoted him for no other reason than to mimic his inimitable voice, we knew he was right.

With all that life proposes and places in our paths, it would be easy to consider ourselves adrift, bumped along aimlessly by what happens to us and the world around us. We ask ourselves, "Where am I headed? Does all this fit into some plan for me, some goal? Will life be merely a string of events with no purpose or destination?" We might begin to think that if indeed we have no final destination, it doesn't matter how we live today.

Modern thought and custom often emphasize the here-and-now as the only ultimate reality, with little reference to long-term implications of present-day decisions. Some people see this as freedom, as setting their own course; but we must have the long view in order to understand and tackle present choices, trials, and temptations. However we might feel about the present moment — set adrift or self-confident — if we do not discover our destiny and set our lives firmly on the road that leads there, we will eventually lose hope and feel utterly alone. If we don't know where we're going, any road will get us there.

Providentially, we do know where we're going. We have a purpose, a goal, a destination, and a destiny — and he is Jesus Christ.

The end of the world is a frequent focus of biblical writers. We should understand the word "end" in two ways: first, referring to the fact that someday this world will literally end; and second, referring to the "goal" or "purpose" of life. Both meanings help us get a handle on the present and teach us that we are not aimlessly adrift, no matter what today's events set before us. Through life's opportunities and trials, united with Christ, our heavenly Father is leading us to eternal life.

Christians don't sit idly in this world, awaiting its literal end. We live now in a way that respects the divine destiny of all creation.

Yes, this world will end; and yes, this world has a goal, a destiny. As St. Paul wrote, everything was created through Christ and for Christ, and everything is destined for Christ. The here-and-now is indeed very important, not on its own merit but precisely because of the destiny God has set for all creation. That destiny is the light with which we can see today, the compass to guide how we live today.

Christians don't sit idly in this world, awaiting its literal end. We live now in a way that respects the divine destiny of all creation — treating each person with the dignity that is his or hers as a child of God; paying special attention to the most vulnerable and to the poor, whom Jesus singles out as especially beloved to him; serving as ambassadors of his peace and working to end conflict wherever we find it; living morally upright lives; growing in holiness through prayer and the sacraments.

These are the ingredients which, when lived out, point us squarely in the direction of the goal of our lives and unveil for us God's presence. These are the ingredients of a hope-filled life because they form a life filled with Christ.

We do not live such a life in a vacuum. We have trials and struggles, some of which can be quite disheartening. Christ helps us see that he is at work even there — quietly, mysteriously, perhaps painfully — but at work nonetheless, showing the way to the resolution of all things in his love.

I find it interesting to read how ancient writers described the reason for hope in the midst of the here-and-now.

St. Macarius wrote:

> Christ ... came to till the soil of mankind devastated by sin. He assumed a body and, using the cross as his plowshare, cultivated the barren soul of man. He removed the thorns and thistles which are the evil spirits and pulled up the weeds of sin.... And when he had plowed the soul with the wood of the cross, he planted in it a most lovely garden of the Spirit, that could produce for its Lord and God the sweetest and most pleasant fruit of every kind.

St. Augustine wrote:

> Let us sing alleluia here on earth, while we still live in anxiety, so that we may sing it one day in heaven in full security.... God is faithful, says holy Scripture, and he will not allow you to be tried beyond your strength.... You have entered upon a time of trial but you will come to no harm — God's help will bring you through it safely. You are like a piece of pottery, shaped by instruction, fired by tribulation.

Jesus is the Way that leads to our destination, and he is that destination. The Church is the bark (ship) of Peter on which we sail along Jesus' Way under the breath of the Holy Spirit. We are his fields, plowed by his cross to sprout the seed that is his word. We are vessels of clay — fragile and prone to break — but made nonetheless by his hand, according to his precise design, and destined to be filled with him forever.

Not adrift at all, but going somewhere — to God, our creator and destiny.

Learning the Art of Seeking God's Will

In his remarks during the National Prayer Breakfast a few years back, the singer Bono recounted that once when undertaking a new charitable outreach, he told a clergyman that he wanted God to bless his efforts. His friend responded, "If you want God to bless your efforts, then get involved in what God is doing — it is already blessed."

An interesting and helpful perspective. Is it best to start a new venture, make a decision, or speak out on an important issue — and then ask God to bless what I have done? Or is it preferable to begin by asking God if it is his will to start that venture, make that decision, or speak out? I think it is the latter.

It is natural for us to hope and pray for good outcomes to what we undertake in life. The question is, when do I begin asking God's perspective?

In some families, a young man seeking to marry a young woman will visit her parents to ask their "blessing." In this case, "blessing" means "approval" of a decision he has already reached. The young man would be happy to receive their approval, but if he does not, he may or may not change his mind about marrying their daughter.

In our dealings with God, we take a different approach. Whatever the issue, we begin by praying, "I want to do your will in this matter, Lord. Help me to know your will." We give to God the entire decision-making process, and thus it is "blessed," because from the outset we are seeking what God wants and sincerely opening ourselves to what he has to say.

How does God respond? In a variety of ways, usually in keeping with our temperament and our willingness to listen patiently

Spiritual masters have always taught that God typically speaks in peace.

and humbly. Spiritual masters have always taught that God typically speaks in peace. In other words, if we experience an inner turbulence as we ponder certain possibilities, that is not the voice of God. He speaks peacefully, and his will settles gently in our hearts. It "fits." What he asks is that we make it our intention — from the very outset — to be obedient to him.

The Latin, Greek, and Hebrew words for "obey" all have to do with "listening carefully" or "paying close attention." Obedience is about listening to God's word and submitting ourselves to it. We may have a tendency to think that seeking God's will is something we do occasionally when faced with a particular challenge or decision, but that is not the case. Seeking God's will is something we are to do every day, so that every activity and every movement of our hearts is blessed. When the occasion arises that we must face a challenge or make a decision, our ears are already turned toward God, for our orientation is habitually that of seeking his will.

Most of the time we will hear no voice and receive no lightning bolt in answer to prayer for God's guidance. However, looking for such signs is not the point. The point is to submit the question to God, empty myself of the desire to do only what I want, open myself to God's intervention, and desire to be obedient to him. I can then go about using the criteria one normally uses in making decisions, trusting that I have placed the whole affair in his hands and that he will guide me as he sees fit.

At times, God does not give a clear indication of his will, and he may prefer to remain quiet for his own reasons. It might be his will that we decide for ourselves! If so, he will bring good out of whatever happens.

God wants us to seek only good, but he does not want us to torment ourselves by gruelingly searching for absolute certainty in a way that only increases our anxiety and distracts us from listening quietly to him. St. Faustina offered good advice in this regard:

> When one does not know what is best, one must reflect, consider, and take counsel, because one does not have the right to act in incertitude of conscience. [If the incertitude remains] one must tell oneself: Whatever I do, it will be good, provided that I have the intention to do good.... Don't be chagrined if, after a certain time, you see that these things are not good. God looks at the intention with which we begin....

God does not want us to be filled with anxiety. We hand over to him our hearts, our desires, our ears, and our wills — practicing daily — and he will not fail us. I recently came across a prayer by Father Jacques Philippe that puts things in perspective:

> Lord, I have thought about it and prayed to know your will. I do not see it clearly, but I am not going to trouble myself any further. I am not going to spend hours racking my brain. I am deciding such and such a thing because, all things carefully considered, it seems to me the best thing to do. And I leave everything in your hands. I know well that, even if I am mistaken, you will not be displeased with me, for I have acted with good intentions. And if I have made a mistake, I know that you are able to draw good from this error. It will be for me a source of humility and I will learn something from it!

Amen.

Christian Stewardship Is a Response to God's Generosity

When I was pastor of a parish in Memphis, Tennessee, our church underwent a months-long renovation project, during which we celebrated Sunday Mass in the social hall. It happened that during that period I was asked to officiate at the wedding of some friends from another parish. I was happy to accommodate them at our place, and they did not mind the temporary arrangement.

It was a simple, joyful celebration. Back in the makeshift sacristy after the wedding, I detected the roar of a vacuum cleaner coming from the hall. I peeked out the door, and sure enough, there was the father of the bride, a Colombian immigrant, vacuuming the floor.

"What are you doing, Jaime?" I asked.

"Vacuuming the floor," came the response.

"How did you find our vacuum cleaner?"

"This one is mine. I brought it from home."

That simple encounter taught me a great deal about Jaime and about stewardship. He was so respectful of the property of others and grateful for being allowed to use it that he went beyond the call of duty to care for it as if it were his own. His gesture was also an expression of respect for the thousands of others who use the facility.

Yes, parish facilities are built with parishioners' money, but in a truer sense they are built with what belongs to God, the tithe of good stewards. They are gifts to be treated with respect and care, as one would care for his or her own home — or better yet, as one would care for someone else's home.

Even those things I "own" are ultimately not truly mine but gifts from God to be shared.

The vast majority of Catholics enjoy worship and parish life in facilities they did not pay for. Even if at present we happen to be members of a new or expanding parish and have contributed to a building campaign, we were probably reared in a parish where the facilities were handed down from past generations. We all enjoy the fruit of the blood, sweat, tears, and generosity of our forebears; and we have a responsibility to hand on to future generations the fruit of our generosity. In doing so, we are only acknowledging that everything comes from the hand of God and belongs to him. An ancient Hebrew insight teaches that almsgiving restores God's right order in the world, for through it we use his gifts according to his plan.

The foregoing is equally true of our stewardship of creation and the way we care for the environment. The care I give my surroundings — my room, my office, my neighborhood, my parish, the park I enjoy, and the roads I travel — is a sign both of gratitude to God and respect for neighbors.

A proper understanding of stewardship reminds me that even those things I "own" are ultimately not truly mine but gifts from God to be shared. The great Rabbi Abraham Heschel once wrote, "What we own, we owe."

A tithe — a "gift" to one's church — is merely a response to God's generosity, recognition that the standard for giving is set by him who holds back nothing from us. As St. Paul wrote to the Corinthians, "What do you possess that you have not received? But if you have received it, why are you boasting as if you did not receive it?" (1 Corinthians 4:7). We humbly admit that even our "hard-earned money" is a gift from God.

We would do well to take a gauge of our stewardship: the way we treat personal property and the property of others; the gratitude we show for the privilege of having parish facilities at our disposal; the strings — the control — we sometimes attach to our financial stewardship, as if we have bought something rather than made a gift; the initiative we take in maintaining parish facilities, whether or not we were the ones who dirtied them; and the humility with which we acknowledge God as the giver of everything.

Being good stewards also means developing sensitivity to the needs of others and recognizing that in Christ they are our brothers and sisters who deserve our loving attention and assistance. We have all been the beneficiaries of the anonymous generosity of those who came before us and those who surround us now, and giving is a concrete way of expressing thanksgiving:

> Bring the whole tithe
>   into the storehouse,
> That there may be food in my house.
>   Put me to the test, says the LORD of hosts,
> And see if I do not open the floodgates of heaven for you,
>   and pour down upon you blessing without measure!
> (Malachi 3:10)

Learning to be good stewards stretches us to appreciate with greater and greater thanksgiving just how good God is to us. Good stewards discover that giving in imitation of God's generosity brings them great joy!

A few months ago I returned to Memphis to visit family and friends, and I had the privilege of baptizing my great-nephew, Diego. He is the son of my niece, Mary, and her husband, David — who happens to be Jaime's son! I had no idea when I married those friends in my parish church years ago that the father of the bride would one day also be the father-in-law of my niece. As we finished the reception following the baptism, my sister nudged me and pointed to Jaime. He was cleaning the tops of the tables, making sure we left the parish hall in tip-top shape.

Signs That We Belong to Christ

I recently revived a small personal tradition my parents taught us when we were small — to make the sign of the cross each time I hear the siren of an ambulance or police car. It is a small gesture, but it carries great significance.

Why did my parents teach us to do that? They wanted us to know that the blare of a siren not only rattles our nerves and pains our ears — it also signals that someone is in trouble and needs our prayers. Making the sign of the cross, we ask God to look after the person, and we remind ourselves never to be indifferent to suffering. Most of the time the siren passes by at breakneck speed and is forgotten, but even more often we pass suffering persons in the hallway or walking down the street. There is no siren, but lines of worry across their brows hint at their pain and draw us to love them. My parents wanted us to learn to notice those who need us.

I think my parents had another motivation in teaching this simple tradition: They wanted us to be comfortable making public expressions of our Catholic faith. We rarely ate at restaurants, but when we did we began with the sign of the cross and a prayer, just as we did at home — publicly saying we were a Catholic family, that we belonged to Jesus Christ.

I don't recall when I stopped making the sign of the cross when a siren passed, but I have a feeling it had something to do with embarrassment at such a public gesture of faith. To be honest, it is embarrassing now to write those words. How could I ever be embarrassed to send a signal that I belong to Christ?

One of the wonderful aspects of being Catholic is that small gestures and signs link daily life with our faith in Jesus Christ —

> *In shying away from making the sign of the cross in public, I was shying away from Christ.*

the sign of the cross, the crucifix on the wall of our home, the family prayer before dinner, the visit to the cemetery, the bow, the genuflection, the rosary in our pockets, the ashes on our foreheads. These are public signs — and while they do proclaim to others that we belong to Christ, they first of all serve as reminders to us that we belong to him.

It dawned on me, for example, that in shying away from making the sign of the cross in public, I was shying away from Christ, creating a separation between my faith in him and the events of each day. He is with me, within me, at every moment, and the more I remind myself of his presence and his grace, the better I will follow him and live my faith in the simple opportunities that life constantly brings me. If I hesitate to proclaim, even in small ways, that I belong to Christ, what am I saying to him?

A critical aspect of living our faith in Jesus Christ is that by doing so we have an effect on the world — we change the environment in which we live. It is not a matter of drawing attention to ourselves, hitting others over the head with our faith, or imposing it on them. It is a matter of giving witness to the presence of Christ and allowing him to use us as his instruments. It is a matter of making room for him in our homes, our workplaces, and our communities. It is a matter of humbly allowing him to guide our actions and our words. It is a matter of belief that he is the Savior of the world, and that he sends us to proclaim him, to live our faith in him.

The *Letter to Diognetus*, a second-century Christian document, put it this way:

> The Christian is to the world what the soul is to the body.... It is by the soul, enclosed within the body, that

> the body is held together.... Such is the Christian's lofty and divinely appointed function, from which he is not permitted to excuse himself.

There is a huge variety of public expressions of faith, and I use the example of the sign of the cross simply as a starting point for reflection. The greatest public expression of faith is love. We Christians know that our love — lived publicly and privately, in ways great and small — has as its origin Jesus Christ, whose disciples and instruments we are. It is he who loves through us. It is he who draws others to himself through us.

"I have been crucified with Christ; yet I live, no longer I, but Christ lives in me; insofar as I now live in the flesh, I live by faith in the Son of God who has loved me and given himself up for me" (Galatians 2:19-20).

When we find ourselves shying away from publicly expressing our faith in Jesus Christ, we can remind ourselves: He will never shy away from us.

"Always be ready to give an explanation to anyone who asks you for a reason for your hope, but do it with gentleness and reverence" (1 Peter 3:15-16).

Christ is our hope!

Searching Beyond the Best

No doubt about it, my aunt Pat Poole made the best angel food cake in the world.

Alma Sangilantoni, a neighbor when I was a kid in Memphis, made the best ravioli and gravy in the world (in the South, Italians call sauce "gravy").

Radefeld's Bakery in the shopping center down the street from our house fried the best doughnuts in the world.

Seesel's Supermarket in Memphis had the best meat.

My sister Sally makes the best biscuits.

And Anne Miller of Westmont, Illinois, bakes the best brownies. In the world.

Granted, I have not been everywhere in the world, but that does not stop me from making judgments about what is the "best in the world." The search for the best, however, has its hazards.

A few years ago, I stopped searching for the best razor in the world because of a shaving mishap. I have a heavy beard, though it is now mostly white, and when I was younger I always seemed to have a five o'clock shadow, even in the morning. Razors first had one blade, then two, then three, then four, and I reasoned that with more blades I would get a better shave. My theory broke down at two blades, but that didn't stop me from trying three and four.

Greeting parishioners of the cathedral in Little Rock after Mass one Sunday, I noticed a man waiting off to the side and sporting a big grin. Eventually, he made his way over and, eyeing the Band-Aid on my upper lip, said, "I see you tried one of those new razors with four blades." He was on target (for he had done the same), and thus my search for the perfect razor ended that Sunday morning. I went back to two blades.

Searching relentlessly for the best can lead to excess and illusion.

All of us search for the best, make judgments about the best, and hope for the best. On the face of it, there is nothing wrong with doing so. But searching relentlessly for the best can lead to excess and illusion. Moreover, if our search and our judgments and our hopes are based on the assumption that the best this world offers will bring us fulfillment, we will be setting our sights much lower than where God would have us search. The problem is not the search but the category we use in the search.

St. Paul preferred the word "fullness" to describe what God has in store for us, and for him, "fullness" went beyond any "best" we could find in this life:

> So, as you received Christ Jesus the Lord, walk in him, rooted in him and built upon him and established in the faith as you were taught, abounding in thanksgiving. See to it that no one captivate you with an empty, seductive philosophy according to human tradition, according to the elemental powers of the world and not according to Christ.
>
> For in him dwells the whole fullness of the deity bodily, and you share in this fullness in him, who is the head of every principality and power. (Colossians 2:6-10)

> He is the image of the invisible God,
> the firstborn of all creation.
> For in him were created all things in heaven and on earth,
> the visible and the invisible,
> whether thrones or dominions or principalities or
> powers;
> all things were created through him and for him.

He is before all things,
  and in him all things hold together....
For in him all the fullness was pleased to dwell.
(Colossians 1:15-17, 19)

For this reason I kneel before the Father, from whom every family in heaven and on earth is named, that he may grant you in accord with the riches of his glory to be strengthened with power through his Spirit in the inner self, and that Christ may dwell in your hearts through faith; that you, rooted and grounded in love, may have strength to comprehend with all the holy ones what is the breadth and length and height and depth, and to know the love of Christ that surpasses knowledge, so that you may be filled with all the fullness of God.
(Ephesians 3:14-19)

I have a feeling that the prodigal son in Jesus' parable (Luke 15) squandered his inheritance on searching for "the best." His resources exhausted, heavy-footed, and ashamed, he returned home. There his father lavished him with love — the same love he had always bestowed on both sons: the extraordinary, full love, of which the monetary inheritance was but a pale reflection. Equally shortsighted as his repentant brother, the elder son protested the lavish welcome; but his father reminded him, "You are here with me always, and everything I have is yours."

We spend a lot of time looking for the best — and more of the best — when we already have in Jesus the fullness of everything. I have a list of "bests," but only he is beyond the best, with whose fullness I long to be filled. Every worthwhile search ends in him.

Surrendering to Jesus' Teaching

Several priests I knew in Arkansas, when poking fun at themselves for making a self-evident point, used to quote the fictional preacher who was fond of saying, "Jesus said, and I tend to agree...."

It's a great line — as if a preacher could ever make himself the judge of Jesus' teaching!

The line makes me laugh, but it also makes me think. I wonder if at times even we Christians approach the teaching of Jesus as something with which we may agree or disagree, as if it is simply one of many philosophies of life among which we may pick and choose as suits our sensibilities.

A modern tendency to give equal weight to all ideas and opinions has a subtle but devastating effect on the Christian life because it seduces us into thinking that there is no such thing as absolute truth. If we think there is no such thing as absolute truth, we will never truly believe that Jesus is the Son of God and Savior of the world. In line with modern habits, we might judge Christian teaching to be acceptable, reasonable, or even appealing — but that's a far cry from actually being a Christian.

The mission of God's Son was not to teach a philosophy but to reveal the Truth so that we might be saved. He himself is the Truth, the absolute Truth. He is God's complete revelation of himself. "Whoever has seen me has seen the Father," he said to Philip (John 14:9). And Paul wrote to the Colossians, "He is the image of the invisible God" (Colossians 1:15). His teachings unveiled the truth, but so did his mercy, his love, his healings, and his miracles. The revelation of truth in Jesus came to its climax in his complete outpouring of himself in his death, resurrection, ascension, and the sending of the Holy Spirit. Jesus calls us to hear, believe, and live the truth so that we might understand and love him, so that through him we might gain the eternal life for which we are destined. We will never know ourselves unless we look at ourselves in the light of his truth.

We will never know ourselves unless we look at ourselves in the light of his truth.

I have a sneaking suspicion that if we were to scrutinize our knee-jerk opinions under the light of the Gospel, we would find some that do not "agree" with Jesus. Still, we cling to such opinions, ignore the glaring discrepancy, consider our position superior, and leave honest self-examination to another day. It's as if we are saying, "Jesus said, but I tend to disagree…." It's unthinkable that a Christian would say such a thing, but perhaps we do just that, and more often than we would like to admit.

If we are Christian, we are not judges of Jesus but disciples who accept him as the Truth who sheds light on every aspect of our lives. For the Christian, there can be no hidden corner of life that does not belong to Jesus, which we are not willing to hand over to him. There can be no opinion or idea that we are not willing to scrutinize in the light of the Gospel.

There is no denying that it is not easy to be Jesus' disciples, to understand all his teaching, and to die to ourselves. Surrendering ourselves to him is a lifelong process, through which we are tried, stretched, molded, and challenged. If we unwittingly set ourselves up as his judges by ignoring the truth he has revealed or allowing ourselves to disagree with him, we will never know him, and we will never find peace and fulfillment.

It seems to me that one of the most serious downfalls of modern culture is its lack of humility. In a certain sense, modern culture has set itself up as the only competent judge of all things, the underlying assumption being that because we know more than we did in the past, we also "know better." We presume that our knowledge gives us a kind of superiority. We are accustomed to being the judge: "Prove it." "Convince me." "I agree with that." "I don't agree with that." Such expectations and judgments have their place, but not in our relationship with God. Spiritually, they might be nothing more than outward manifestations of inflated egos, hard hearts, or fear.

Faith in God demands the humble admission that we are neither gods, nor judges, nor ends in ourselves. Faith in God demands that we humbly surrender our lives to him who alone is truth. Faith in God demands that we assent to his way as the only way for which we were created. Faith in God calls not for convincing but for conversion.

Humility is the hoe that softens our hearts so that God's word, God's Truth, can take root in us. Humility is actually a facet of courage that enables us to hand over to God any opinions, ideas, and behaviors which do not agree with the truth. We are all afraid of change, but the kind of change to which Jesus calls us never disappoints.

Defined by God's Desires

"To live means to be desired and loved
by God, moment after moment."
(Jubilee of the Consecrated Life)

Of all the ways one might define human life, that brief and startling statement says everything. I wonder what kind of definition each of us would write were we asked to define "to live." I have a suspicion that many of us would begin, "To live means that I …" Our definitions would continue with a list of things that "I" would accomplish, achieve, feel, think, know, do.

But the true definition does not begin with anything that I set as a goal for myself. Instead, it begins with recognizing that the only reason I am alive is that I am "desired and loved by God." By desiring and loving me, God brought me into being and sustains me. I am neither the source nor the goal of my own life. I am one who is desired and loved by God, moment after moment, and therefore I am alive. My existence is evidence that God exists!

For most of us, taking that definition seriously means letting a revolution happen in our hearts. If the reason I am alive is that I am a desire of God, the beloved of God, a thought of God, an object of God's favor, then nourishing a relationship with God brings me even more to life. Making myself the center, the point of it all, only lessens me.

It is the revolutionary irony of the Gospel that in forgetting myself I find myself, that in surrendering myself to God as his instrument I come alive. That upside-down logic is emphasized by the Gospels as a key to Jesus' teaching: "For whoever wishes to save his life will lose it, but whoever loses his life for my sake will save it. What profit is there for one to gain the whole world yet lose or forfeit himself?" (Luke 9:24-25).

"What does God *call me to do?" That is the proper question to ask oneself when contemplating a vocation.*

One obstacle to serious consideration of a religious vocation is that we begin by asking, "Should *I* do this?" In other words, we approach a vocation as we would a career change, when, in fact, it has much more to do with our willingness to leap into God's arms. It has to do with surrendering ourselves to the truth — even though we do not fully understand it — that no matter what I have already accomplished, the reason I am living is that I am desired and loved by God.

"What does *God* call me to do?" That is the proper question to ask oneself when contemplating a vocation. Discerning a vocation means allowing myself to be defined by God's desire and love for me, to want to become an image of God's love and desire for everyone. In this age of "self-fulfillment," that is no easy task, but it is precisely what the Church — the world — needs.

Discerning a vocation means putting myself at God's disposal, so that when he calls I will not respond, "I have something better to do."

Am I afraid of falling? God will catch me. Am I too weak? Yes, but God is strong. Will I miss my former life? Perhaps, but I will gain something more. Will I abandon what I have built up? No, I will give it to God. Will I lose my family? No, I will grow even closer to them, and God will even expand my family. Will I limit my future choices? Most definitely yes, but in giving myself to God I will gain everything.

Please join me in prayer for those who are considering a vocation to the priesthood or religious life (and for those who are not considering a vocation but should be!). Pray that they will come alive in God's desire and love for them, that they will give their "I" to God for his sake and ours. Pray that they will have the courage to stake their lives on what it means "to live." Pray that they will hear his call and answer, "Yes!"

Am I an Admirer or a Follower?

There were many who observed Jesus closely as he went about his business. Some knew him as a lifelong friend and neighbor, some as a local tradesman like so many others. There were those who knew of his devotion to his widowed mother, while others recalled his quiet fidelity to the law and things spiritual.

One day he left the obscure security of home and trade and began to speak publicly of his Father, to beckon others to the truth that something new was happening. He not only told them about this new life, he showed it to them — and many took notice. They found him fascinating, his words appealing, and his miracles tantalizing and even persuasive.

They observed hangers-on accompanying him on his walks around town and across desert roads to the next towns, and some wondered if it wouldn't be interesting actually to go on one of those walks. Others watched from their front porches, knowing his name but not really knowing him. Some asked friends if it were even worthwhile to give him the time of day, while others simply ignored him as one more in a succession of teachers who had come and gone over the years.

Many admired him.

They admired his welcoming demeanor, his smile, his peaceful spirit. They admired his lessons about spendthrift sons and merciful fathers, about seeds sown carelessly and weeds thriving stubbornly, about wedding banquets and the hungry poor and about lost things and just judgments. Who could not identify with such colorful imagery from lives they lived, people they knew, and earth they plowed?

They watched God's power at work in him: The man who had been blind his whole life could now see, and the troubled man who used to beg by the gate could now hold down a job and feed his family. There were rumors of a little girl who at his touch had awakened from death and a friend of his who walked out of the tomb three days after death when Jesus called his name.

No doubt about it, he struck a nerve, and something within them listened and yearned for more. Still, there were troubling things too.

There was glorious talk of God forgiving the worst of sins, but there was also the implication that we are to forgive just as magnanimously. He said that in order to find our lives we would have to lose them, but how could that be possible? He insinuated that there are crosses to carry and that he himself would die on one and then rise — but how could he be our Savior if he died? And whoever heard of resurrection from the dead? There was crazy talk about eating his flesh and drinking his blood, and it was well known that many of his admirers walked away when he said such things. He even claimed to be God's only Son — and if that were true, well, everything had changed.

It could be a good thing to listen to him, to put into practice some of his lessons; but to accept him without question, to let go of one's own approach and one's own opinions — well, that was another thing altogether!

Many admired him, but only some followed him. Danish philosopher Søren Kierkegaard wrote:

> What, then, is the difference between an admirer and a follower? A follower is or strives to be what he admires. An admirer, however, keeps himself personally detached. He fails to see that what is admired involves a claim upon him, and thus he fails to be or strive to be what he admires....
>
> The admirer never makes any true sacrifices. He always plays it safe. Though in word he is inexhaustible about how highly he prizes Christ, he renounces noth-

ing, will not reconstruct his life, and will not let his life express what it is he supposedly admires. No, no. The follower aspires with all his strength to be what he admires.

There were those in Jesus' own day who knew him well and liked what he did and said but never followed him, who never became his disciples. Do we sometimes live as admirers yet hold back from giving him everything? Do we clutch tenaciously, even if unwittingly, to our stubborn will or to ways of living opposed to the ways of God? Are we too afraid or selfish to give him everything and to confess that we have sinned?

Do we sometimes live as admirers yet hold back from giving him everything?

You and I don't find it any easier to follow Jesus than did countless Christians who have gone before us. Just like them, however, we can take courage in his unfailing fidelity to us, his patience and his mercy, as we aspire with all our strength to become true disciples and not just admirers.

An admirer can walk away, because there is no real attachment. As Jesus watched some of his admirers leave him because they found his teaching hard (see John 6:60-71), he thought sadly about what they were giving up. He said to the Twelve, "Do you also want to leave?" Each new day in our lives of faith provides us with opportunities to renounce what does not belong to his ways, to abandon everything, to resolve to stay with him permanently, and to allow him to reconstruct us by his grace.

He knows we have more to hand over to him, and we know that he alone has the words of eternal life.

Each of Our Days Is in God's Hands

The Liturgy of the Hours ends each Monday night with a prayer that never fails to catch my attention:

> Lord,
> give our bodies restful sleep
> and let the work we have done today
> bear fruit in eternal life.

It is always good for me to take stock of the fact that somehow what I do each day plays a part in God's plan and through him can bear fruit for me and for others in eternal life. Because it is easy to fall into the trap of assuming that only the projects I complete and the goals I accomplish bear fruit, God invites me to broaden my horizons. He asks me, "Do you believe that your life matters to me, that I have included you in my plan? Are you willing to recognize that everything you do in the course of a day participates in my plan, even activities which seem to be of no consequence, even those which seem to have failed or leave you perplexed and fearful?"

In his love and providence, God uses us in ways far beyond our understanding, and what we do each moment matters to him and serves his purpose. God depends neither on our success nor on our awareness of exactly how we are serving as his instruments. In fact, he does not even define "success" as we do. He can bring fruit from a humdrum daily routine, the smallest step we take, and even our failures. He simply asks that we cooperate with him by trying our best to follow his ways.

Does God use only people of influence to execute his plan? If we do not have a position of importance or hold some measure of power, are we of any use to him? Are there certain aspects of our lives that matter to him but others about which he cares little?

Jesus answers such questions quite clearly:

> "Are not five sparrows sold for two small coins? Yet not one of them has escaped the notice of God. Even the hairs of your head have all been counted. Do not be afraid. You are worth more than many sparrows." (Luke 12:6-7)

Not only is each of us of incalculable value to God — he has a plan for us, one that matters a great deal to him, to us, and to others; and each moment of our lives participates in that plan.

He has a plan for us, one that matters a great deal to him, to us, and to others.

Blessed John Henry Cardinal Newman, a nineteenth-century convert from Anglicanism to Catholicism, once wrote:

> I have a place in God's counsels, in God's world, which no one else has; whether I be rich or poor, despised or esteemed by man, God knows me and calls me by my name. God has created me to do him some definite service. He has committed some work to me which he has not committed to another. I have my mission. I may never know it in this life, but I shall be told it in the next. I am a link in a chain, a bond of connection between persons. He has not created me for naught. I shall do good; I shall do his work. I shall be an angel of peace, a preacher of truth in my own place, while not intending it, if I do but keep his commandments and serve him in my calling.
>
> Therefore, I will trust him. Whatever, wherever I am, I can never be thrown away. If I am in sickness, my sickness may serve him; in perplexity, my perplexity may serve him. If I am in sorrow, my sorrow may serve him.

> He does nothing in vain.... He may take away my friends. He may throw me among strangers. He may make me feel desolate, make my spirits sink, hide the future from me — still, he knows what he is about.

Even if we do not understand clearly God's plan for us, and even if the moments in our day seem so scattered as to follow no rhyme or reason, we can hand ourselves over to him. We can seek at each moment to act as he would have us act, let go of our need to control each minute, and put everything in his hands. As we prepare for bed, we can rest assured that he has lovingly used our day for good.

Edith Stein (St. Teresa Benedicta of the Cross), a convert from Judaism who died at Auschwitz, offers further reflection for the evening:

> When night comes, and you look back over the day and see how fragmentary everything has been, and how much you planned that has gone undone, and all the reasons you have to be embarrassed and ashamed, just take everything exactly as it is, put it in God's hands and leave it with him. Then you will be able to rest in him — really rest — and start the next day as a new life.

The knowledge that each of our days is in God's hands, that each plays a part in his plan, gives us strength and hope. I pray for the wisdom to see things as he sees them and the generosity to work with him, though I may not always be aware how I am doing so. I pray that somehow what I do each day will bear fruit now and in eternal life.

CHAPTER 2

KEEPING OUR PERSPECTIVE ALONG THE WAY

Grounded in God's Strength

To say the least, the old photograph you see on the opposite page falls into the "Don't try this at home" category, but I have always enjoyed looking at it. Taken almost one hundred years ago, most likely it depicts one of my father's elder brothers in their East Tennessee hometown.

What was he thinking? Dangerous, to be sure, and I'll bet my grandparents would have been none too happy to see him pulling such a risky stunt — but still the photo makes me smile. Seemingly oblivious to the danger of high voltage and high altitude, my uncle's facial expression is calm, even stoic; and his feet are at right angles to his legs, as if he were standing on the ground. It would have been impossible for him to hold such a pose for long.

He was literally "hanging on" for dear life, and the weight of his own body was pulling him down. It was as if he were having a battle with himself! What kept him safe for the few moments he posed for the picture was the sheer strength of his grip and nothing more. What a foolish prank, never to be repeated.

As I have studied the photo through the years, I have seen a simple lesson emerge from my uncle's foolishness: Do we some times just "hang on" throughout life, relying on our own grip, our own strength, to keep us safe? Do we think that is what God expects of us?

Faith offers a better, safer, and more "grounded" alternative: We are not to "hang on" but be "planted" in the Lord, "rooted" in *his* strength. When, instead of merely hanging on through life's challenges, we dig more deeply into the Lord, we prosper spiritually, we hold firm through life's storms, and we build a foundation on solid truth and not on attractive but flimsy philosophies.

When we are rooted in God, we truly come alive and prosper.

When we are rooted in God, we truly come alive and prosper; his grace is our strength:

Blessed is the man who does not walk
in the counsel of the wicked,
Nor stand in the way of sinners,
nor sit in company with scoffers.
Rather, the law of the LORD is his joy;
and on his law he meditates day and night.
He is like a tree
planted near streams of water,
that yields its fruit in season;
Its leaves never wither;
whatever he does prospers. (Psalm 1:1-3)

The just shall flourish like the palm tree,
shall grow like a cedar of Lebanon.
Planted in the house of the LORD,
they shall flourish in the courts of our God.
They shall bear fruit even in old age,
they will stay fresh and green.... (Psalm 92:13-15)

> [C]onsider that you do not support the root; the root supports you. (see Romans 11:16-18)

When we are rooted in God, we can hold firm and weather life's storms:

> Thus says the Lord:
> … Blessed are those who trust in the Lord;
> the Lord will be their trust.
> They are like a tree planted beside the waters
> that stretches out its roots to the stream:
> It does not fear heat when it comes,
> its leaves stay green;
> In the year of drought it shows no distress,
> but still produces fruit. (see Jeremiah 17:5-8)

> "Everyone who listens to these words of mine and acts on them will be like a wise man who built his house on rock. The rain fell, the floods came, and the winds blew and buffeted the house. But it did not collapse; it had been set solidly on rock." (Matthew 7:24-25)

When we are rooted in God, our foundation is built on firm truth and not on flimsy philosophies:

> And you who once were alienated and hostile in mind because of evil deeds he has now reconciled in his fleshly body through his death, to present you holy, without blemish, and irreproachable before him, provided that you persevere in the faith, firmly grounded, stable, and not shifting from the hope of the gospel that you heard, which has been preached to every creature under heaven. (Colossians 1:21-23)

> I say this so that no one may deceive you by specious arguments.... So, as you received Christ Jesus the Lord, walk in him, rooted in him and built upon him and established in the faith as you were taught, abounding in thanksgiving. See to it that no one captivate you with an empty, seductive philosophy according to human tradition, according to the elemental powers of the world and not according to Christ. (Colossians 2:4, 6–8)

If we are to cling to anything, we are to cling to Christ. Clinging to him is nothing like "hanging on," for he is shelter and safety, hope and strength, food and drink, root and foundation, wisdom and life. After all, his cross — our tree of life — was firmly planted in the ground.

God Wants Us to Soar

Since arriving in Washington, I have spent many hours on I-5 traveling to the northern and southern reaches of the archdiocese, and like all Washingtonians, I have had many opportunities to watch road construction projects. I admit there is much of the kid left in me, and I am fascinated by cranes, tractors, paving machines, earth movers, excavators, bulldozers, and pile drivers. A particular memory often comes to mind.

One Saturday morning when I was about eight and a Cub Scout, our pack sponsored a kite competition on the soon-to-open leg of I-55 that ran through our neighborhood in Memphis. Kites had to be homemade, and mine was crafted of two slender, flexible dowels with sturdy brown paper glued to the string, that created a diamond-shaped frame. My kite was clumsy, but it took to the air with ease. What created the excitement for us kids, much more than the competition, was that we had permission to run with abandon on a brand-spanking-new I-55 before any vehicle dirtied it. I didn't win the competition, and I don't remember who did. What I remember is running free on I-55.

To be honest, I feel my share of aggravation confronting construction on I-5, most often when I am late for an event and get caught in slow-moving traffic. The fault is entirely mine, of course, but there are times when frustration gets the best of me.

Negotiating heavy, slow-moving traffic one afternoon, I gained a sudden change in perspective from a thoughtful passenger. Observing the busy freeway, he said, "Isn't it marvelous how they are able to keep the road open in the midst of construction?"

In the bedlam of rush-hour traffic, I learned a simple but valuable lesson. Because I had tried to jam too much activity into too few hours, I began to perceive the construction as an obstacle, someone else's "fault," someone else's miscalculation. But my companion saw it differently, and from then on so did I. "Isn't it marvelous how they're able to keep the road open in the midst of construction?"

A particular lesson God never tires of teaching me is to trust him.

A simple change in perspective makes all the difference when it comes to our mood, our worries, our frustrations, or our plans. It amazes me that this is a lesson I must learn over and over again. Half full or half empty? An obstacle or an opportunity? A step backward or a lesson in patience?

A particular lesson God never tires of teaching me is to trust him. Repeatedly, he has given me evidence of his presence and his care, but there are times I let worry take control. It's as if I have amnesia, as if I have forgotten all he has done for me time after time after time. Years ago I read that a good antidote to worry is simply to remember — to call to mind past instances when we were in a real jam (and not just a traffic jam), confronting a problem that seemed to have no solution, and God pulled us through. Remembering, we recall that God has never let us down but helped us mature through thorny situations. Were they difficult? Yes, they were. Did I enjoy them? No, I did not. But would I trade what I learned from them, would I give up the love God showed me through them? Not for a moment.

Simple changes in perspective can change everything. This is most especially true when we seek to join our perspective to God's:

> Be patient, therefore, brothers, until the coming of the Lord. See how the farmer waits for the precious fruit of the earth, being patient with it until it receives the early and the late rains. (James 5:7)

But do not ignore this one fact, beloved, that with the Lord one day is like a thousand years and a thousand years like one day. The Lord does not delay his promise, as some regard "delay," but he is patient with you, not wishing that any should perish but that all should come to repentance. (2 Peter 3:8-9)

"Therefore I tell you, do not worry about your life.... Can any of you by worrying add a single moment to your life-span? ... If God so clothes the grass of the field ... will he not much more provide for you...?
... Seek first the kingdom [of God] and his righteousness, and all these things will be given you besides."
(see Matthew 6:25-33)

Why, O Jacob, do you say,
 and declare, O Israel,
"My way is hidden from the LORD,
 and my right is disregarded by my God"?
Do you not know?
 Have you not heard?
The LORD is God from of old,
 creator of the ends of the earth.
He does not faint or grow weary,
 and his knowledge is beyond scrutiny.
He gives power to the faint,
 abundant strength to the weak.
Though young men faint and grow weary,
 and youths stagger and fall,
They that hope in the LORD will renew their strength,
 they will soar on eagles' wings;
They will run and not grow weary,
 walk and not grow faint. (see Isaiah 40:25-31)

By the grace of God, I am learning that it is not my kite that God wishes to take flight. It is I myself whom he wishes to see soar with freedom like an eagle, having placed everything in his hands.

Love Places Those Dear to Us in God's Heart

When my father died in 1972, I was nineteen and away at college. Although I still returned home for holidays and summer vacations, I had essentially already "moved out." The same was true of two of my four sisters, and within a few years we were all on our own. That went for Mom, too.

In what must have seemed to her the blink of an eye, Mom transitioned from a full house to an empty house. At first, it was very difficult for her, but after a while she grew to like it; and toward the end of her life the decision to move to assisted living was very upsetting — in part because she would no longer live alone.

I have a hunch that Mom, as many aging parents, had to come to terms with two aspects of the solitude of later life: living in a quiet house without the constant conversation of sons, daughters, and grandkids; and feeling somewhat helpless, because now that her kids had moved out on their own, she could no longer protect them as she could when they were young. All of this was a struggle for Mom in both respects, for our family was large and our house had often been the neighborhood gathering place; and as we kids got older, we had our share of experiences to cause her worry.

When I was in my late twenties, the significance of this tender reality began to sink through my thick head. On retreat one year, I visited a religious gift shop and noticed a framed calligraphy of a touching prayer. The prayer gave me insight into Mom's life, so I bought it and left it on her kitchen table one day while she was at work:

By handing us over to the care of Jesus and his mother in prayer, she still held us under her care as well.

> Holy Angels, guardians of my children, you know that I can no longer guard or protect them as I did when they were young. I beg you, with a mother's heart, to protect my children in body and soul. Strengthen their wills, that they may avoid evil. You see the face of our Heavenly Father: ask Him, please, to lead them along the way to goodness, so that someday, together with you, we may sing His praise forever. Amen.

Mom was a woman of few words when it came to receiving gifts, but I could tell she liked it. The prayer immediately went up on the hallway wall near the gallery of family photos. It accompanied Mom to the assisted-living facility a few months before her death in 2005.

Through the years, Mom had learned that although her kids were no longer directly under her roof, we were still under her care. We were a telephone call away, a few miles away — in that sense we were still relatively close by. But we were also on our own, making decisions and plans, caring for our own families — and in that sense we were no longer directly under her protection. What Mom had learned, however — and what she taught us — was that by handing us over to the care of Jesus and his mother in prayer, she still held us under her care as well, deeply and powerfully so.

I thought of this the other night while reading *Interior Freedom* by Father Jacques Philippe. Father Philippe describes the experience of powerlessness known to many people, especially parents, when caring for those we love: At times, we watch as they stumble and fall, all the while realizing we cannot intervene to stop the pain or help in any way. Father Philippe's words are worth quoting:

> At such times we should tell ourselves that even if we apparently have no way of intervening, we still, despite everything, can continue to believe, hope, and love. We can believe that God will not abandon our child and our prayer will bear fruit in due course. We can hope in the Lord's faithfulness and power for everything. We can love by continuing to carry that person in our heart and prayer, forgiving him and forgiving the wrong done to him; and expressing love in every way available to us, including trust, self-abandonment, and forgiveness.
>
> The more devoid of means our love is, the purer and greater it is. Even when, externally, there is nothing to be done, we still have inner freedom to continue to love. No circumstance, however tragic, can rob us of that.... Even if we can do nothing, as long as we believe, hope, and love, something is happening whose fruits will appear sooner or later, in the time of God's mercy.

An aging parent's love for his or her children is a purified love, a love that has fewer physical means at its disposal, but a love that is stronger precisely because it has no "means" to rely on and thus hands everyone over to God. That is also a crucial lesson for me to learn as a bishop.

After Mom died, one of my sisters gave me a prayer card she found in her missal. On the back, Mom had written the words of St. Alphonsus Liguori (the underlining is hers):

> God is all-powerful — he <u>can</u> help. God is good — he wishes to help. God has pledged his word, and he is faithful to his word: therefore he <u>will</u> help.

She added, in her own words: “My Jesus, you are my hope. Mary, my mother, all my confidence rests in you.”

I have no doubt the five of us kids — and later, the grandkids — were the intentions unwritten between the lines.

God Can Use Both Weeds and Wheat

Wheat and weeds grow side by side in all of us.

We will never completely lose the capacity to surprise ourselves with thoughts and emotions that well up spontaneously and fly in the face of our deepest-held values. Just when we think we have forgiven someone, anger resurfaces and we grind our teeth. Just when we think we have conquered our judgmental attitude, we catch ourselves looking askance at a stranger who does not meet our exacting standards. Just when we think we have developed a discipline of prayer, we find ourselves watching a mindless TV show rather than saying good night to the Lord.

We work hard on a fault, do our best to overcome it, but it remains. We turn our lives around, give up the dangerous roads we once traveled, and place our lives completely and sincerely in the hands of God, but old habits haunt us. We joyfully accept God's mercy when we have sinned, only to be surprised by a new fault or frustrated by an unrelenting familiar one.

"Why can't I get it right?" I ask myself. "Why doesn't God notice my sincerity and give me the help I need? Why can't I correct this sin myself? Does the fact that my sins still glare at me mean that I have made no progress? Or am I afraid of being weak, afraid of admitting that I need God?"

Jesus tells a beautiful parable that captures both our fickle nature and God's mysterious ways:

> "The kingdom of heaven may be likened to a man who sowed good seed in his field. While everyone was asleep his enemy came and sowed weeds all through the wheat, and then went off. When the crop grew and bore fruit,

> the weeds appeared as well. The slaves of the householder came to him and said, 'Master, did you not sow good seed in your field? Where have the weeds come from?' He answered, 'An enemy has done this.' His slaves said to him, 'Do you want us to go and pull them up?' He replied, 'No, if you pull up the weeds you might uproot the wheat along with them. Let them grow together until harvest; then at harvest time I will say to the harvesters, "First collect the weeds and tie them in bundles for burning; but gather the wheat into my barn." ' "
> (Matthew 13:24-30)

Wheat and weeds grow side by side in all of us. Faults remain even as we grow spiritually. The devil hopes we will be discouraged by the persistence of the hearty weeds and stop trying to grow spiritually. He does not want us to lean even more on God, because he knows God is ready to help us! For his part, God does not fret about weeds, and he will not do us violence by uprooting weeds and wheat together; he wants us to rely on him and trust that he protects us from any long-term harm the weeds could cause us and will use them somehow for good.

It is important that we unmask a fallacy that often dupes us: the unwitting assumption that whatever "wheat" grows within us is the product of our own effort. Our frustration with weeds, then, stems in part from frustration that we have not been able to wipe them out by ourselves. To unmask the fallacy is to admit that every bit of wheat growing within us is the work of God, and his alone! Remember that the slaves in Jesus' parable asked the householder, "Master, did you not sow good seed in your field?" The seed comes from the hand of the Master, and the wheat grows by his cultivation, not ours.

I like the parable very much because it demonstrates God's patience with the garden — the field — the farm — that is my life. Just as it is he who has caused the wheat to grow, just as it is he who has inspired me to be better, so it is he who sometimes allows weeds to grow alongside wheat and who will use them somehow for my good. Weeds keep me humble! The best thing that could happen is that I will lean more on God and recognize how everything is grace, even those things I thought I had done by myself.

> *Every bit of wheat growing within us is the work of God, and his alone!*

Does the fact that God allows some weeds to remain mean that he somehow "sanctions" such faults? Not at all. God can bring good even out of faults — but that is his work, not mine. Moreover, there is a vast difference between realizing with exasperation that weeds are cropping up, even as we are growing in goodness, and willingly cultivating weeds by our actions and attitudes. What I mean by cultivating weeds is knowingly allowing ourselves to do things that harm us, frequenting places that are not good for us, entering into conversations that will lead us to sin, ignoring opportunities to participate in the sacraments and prayer, and so forth.

If we are willingly cultivating any weed, we can ask God's help to repent and seek only that which nourishes the wheat of goodness and holiness. He asks us to cooperate with what his grace is doing in us, to change and correct what we can — and when those exasperating weeds persist, to lean on him even more, trusting that just as he sowed the good seed, he will prosper the wheat.

Our Patron Saints Choose Us

A long time ago, St. Martin de Porres decided to watch over our family.

My father was born and reared in small-town East Tennessee, where the Catholic population was sparse, to say the least. Paulist priests traveled a circuit by horseback to offer Mass for Catholics spread across a large area.

On January 7, 1912, Father J. Duffy, C.S.P., rode from Winchester to South Pittsburg to baptize Joseph Martin Sartain, born December 30, 1911. He was the son of Luther Benton Sartain Sr. and Josephine Marie Reilly, and the godson of Thomas and Margaret Johnson. I have a photocopy of the page in the makeshift sacramental book, which records the baptism in Latin. The book's tattered pages bear the marks of a priest on the go, one who cared for a far-flung flock, with grit and dedication (even if not with accuracy — he incorrectly listed my father's birthday as December 27).

My father received little in the way of religious education since his mother died when he was a toddler. His father, by then a Catholic, had been reared in the Methodist Church. It was not until after my father married my mother and moved to Memphis in the mid-1940s that he received instructions in the Catholic faith from Father James Driscoll, who remained a family friend until his death on November 12, 1988.

It was apparently during those instructions that the subject of patron saints arose, and my father learned of St. Martin de Porres, whose feast day is November 3. Martin de Porres was born in Lima, Peru, on December 9, 1579, the illegitimate son of a Spanish nobleman and a young freed black slave. He grew up in poverty, and as a boy he spent time with a surgeon-barber, from whom he learned the rudiments of medicine. At age eleven, he became a servant at a Dominican priory, eventually took vows as a Dominican brother, and spent the rest of his life caring for the sick and poor of Lima. He died in 1639.

Their relationship with us is an active one, a two-way street.

No one remembered why our grandparents named our father Martin, but in his mid-thirties he adopted Martin de Porres as his patron. There was always a statue of Martin in our home, we learned about him as we were growing up, and one of my nephews now bears the name.

A priest friend said to me one day that he thinks our patron saints choose us, and I agree completely. They want to help us come close to Jesus. When we speak of the "communion of saints," it is important to reflect on the meaning of "communion." The saints in heaven are one with each other and with us precisely because we are all one in Jesus, and they pray for us that we might grow as disciples and friends of the Lord. They are aware of us before we are aware of them, and just as friends are attracted to one another by similar backgrounds or shared interests, it seems to me that we and the saints have a lot in common. Communion implies relationship, and their relationship with us is an active one, a two-way street.

I imagine St. Martin de Porres chose my father because he was a pharmacist and cared for the sick and downtrodden as Martin had done. Perhaps my father's difficult childhood attracted Martin's attention, for he, too, struggled as a child. Whatever his reasons for choosing him, Martin has been with my family ever since, interceding and watching over us.

This is all the more interesting because my father was known as "Pete," not Martin. I recently discovered a photograph taken of him dressed as a cowboy when he was about five. Because he was fascinated with a character named "Cowboy Pete," he was given a nickname that stuck for life. I was named after that nickname. As a kid playing cowboy in his backyard, my father probably never dreamed he'd have a son named Peter, but I think St. Peter already knew. He would pray for me, that I would be a man who would want to be in union with Jesus.

Through the years, I have also been chosen by St. John of the Cross, St. Teresa of Ávila, St. Thomas More, St. Catherine of Siena, Blessed Pier Giorgio Frassati, and Blessed Karl Leisner. Friends and guides, they know just how I need to grow closer to the Lord. They pray for me and offer inspiration through their writings and example.

In 1912, a circuit-riding Paulist priest brought my father into communion with God's holy ones through Baptism; and when he prayed the Litany of the Saints, Martin de Porres was there, already striking up a friendship with the infant in my grandmother's arms, a friendship that would blossom thirty-something years later.

We are part of an eternal communion in Jesus, and in him we are one with friends seen and unseen. We have more Christian guides and protectors than we imagine, and they are cheering us along the path to life eternal, a path we never travel alone. If you do not have a patron, read the lives of the saints, and one (or more!) will choose you.

Using Words to Build Up (Not to Tear Down)

My father served in the Pacific during World War II. As my mother was moving a few years ago, I came across my father's Pacific scrapbook. I had seen it before, but its contents took on special meaning this time because Mom was leaving her home of forty-six years and because that particular year marked the sixtieth anniversary of the end of World War II.

Telegrams; money-order receipts; train tickets; dinner programs; photographs and drawings; newspapers announcing peace; a copy of *Pacific Leatherneck*, with a feature about Iwo Jima; a letter to my father from James V. Forrestal, Secretary of the Navy, dated October 26, 1945, after my father's formal separation from active military service. It reads, in part: "You have served in the greatest Navy in the world.... No other Navy at any time has done so much. For your part in these achievements you deserve to be proud as long as you live. The Nation which you served at a time of crisis will remember you with gratitude."

My father was deeply proud of his country and his military service until the day he died, and the care with which his Navy memorabilia are stowed is evidence of that pride.

A series of letters to my mother and eldest sister, written almost daily for a week, is also in the scrapbook. Folded carefully together, the letters had apparently been sent as a group. The first begins:

> Dearest Sweethearts: I don't know whether I should write this letter or not. In fact I don't know whether you'll ever get it or not but I wanted to put it all down

> and if I have to carry it with me, maybe I can show it to you someday....

Words, even false words, are powerful.

His ship was on its way to Leyte Island in the Philippines, where a beachhead had been established the previous day. His tanker was to deliver fuel and supplies. He adds:

> Tokyo Rose told us yesterday that 30,000 of our troops have been killed which of course is a lie. She even told us to remember that Christmas presents were on the way for those men which they would never get. She also reminded us that we probably won't get ours. We get a kick out of listening to her. Day before yesterday she told us that our entire third fleet was destroyed. We are part of that fleet and were very much afloat at that time.

Tokyo Rose was the nickname given by GIs to several English-speaking women who spread demoralizing propaganda via radio in the Pacific theater. An American woman was eventually tried and convicted of treason as Tokyo Rose, but President Gerald Ford granted her a full pardon in 1977 because of clear evidence that those who testified against her had perjured themselves. She had wrongly been used as a scapegoat.

My father and his buddies got a kick out of Tokyo Rose's lies, but I have a feeling her repeated reminders that they were far from home and family dug a painful pit into their psyches. Because words, even false words, are powerful, propaganda has often been used in armed conflict to dishearten the opposition. What about our words? In an age of instant communication, I wonder if we sometimes forget the power of our tongue — and our laptop — for good and for ill. The Letter of James offers the metaphor of ships and rudders to explain the power of the tongue:

> Even though [ships] are so large and driven by fierce winds, they are steered by a very small rudder wherever the pilot's inclination wishes. In the same way the tongue is a small member and yet has great pretensions.... With [the tongue] we bless the Lord and Father, and with it we curse human beings who are made in the likeness of God. From the same mouth come blessing and cursing. This need not be so, my brothers. (James 3:4-5, 9-10)

Paul was equally convinced of the power of words. "No foul language should come out of your mouths, but only such as is good for needed edification, that it may impart grace to those who hear" (Ephesians 4:29). A Christian's words should always be for "building up," never for "tearing down." Our words of peace and encouragement can, as Paul writes, give grace to those who hear them.

My father once wrote words of love to my mother and sister, not knowing if they would ever read them. When finally received, those wartime words were so precious to my mother that she carefully preserved them in scrapbooks and boxes. The words of several Tokyo Roses, patently and deliberately false, were aimed at young, homesick American GIs. Words can build up — and they can tear down.

May every one of our words, written and spoken, have as their goal to strengthen, encourage, give hope, and edify. Those who hear us will cherish the strength we give them. May a harsh word or a curse never fall from lips created by God to give him praise.

More on the Power of Words

Among the things forbidden in our house as I was growing up — vulgar, racist, or blasphemous words — was the word "stupid." To be honest, at first it struck me as odd that we were not allowed to use that word, because it seemed fairly benign as words go. I gradually came to realize that it was off-limits because it is a cheap word too easily thrown around to offend or belittle.

The larger lesson was that in addition to words on a forbidden list, there is another serious offense to avoid — the intentional misuse of speech to injure another. Even benign words can injure when strung together in sarcasm.

The etymology of the word "sarcasm" leads back to the Greek *sarkazein*, to tear flesh, to bite one's lips in rage, to sneer. Thus sarcasm is a sharp, sometimes ironic verbal expression designed to ridicule and inflict pain; its effect depends on bitter, caustic, cutting language. My parents were wise to ban such language from our house because they knew that sarcasm injures, divides, and creates an atmosphere of hostility — things poisonous to a family.

It seems to me that a great deal of entertainment humor these days falls in the category of vulgar sarcasm. In other words, it is cheap and adolescent; it poisons; it divides; it injures. New Testament authors, especially James and Paul, point out insistently that such language is antithetical to the dignity of those who follow Christ.

St. James recognized the power of the tongue for evil:

> If we put bits into the mouths of horses to make them obey us, we also guide their whole bodies. It is the same with ships: even though they are so large and driven by fierce winds, they are steered by a very small rudder wherever the pilot's inclination wishes. In the same way the tongue is a small member and yet has great pretensions.

Christ calls us to construct his household with words that build up rather than tear down.

> Consider how small a fire can set a huge forest ablaze. The tongue is also a fire.... For every kind of beast and bird, of reptile and sea creature, can be tamed and has been tamed by the human species, but no human being can tame the tongue. It is a restless evil, full of deadly poison. With it we bless the Lord and Father, and with it we curse human beings who are made in the likeness of God. From the same mouth come blessing and cursing. This need not be so, my brothers. (see James 3)

St. Paul recognized that language misused injures the Body of Christ:

> You must no longer live as the Gentiles do, in the futility of their minds; darkened in understanding, alienated from the life of God because of their ignorance, because of their hardness of heart, they have become callous.... That is not how you learned Christ.... [P]ut on the new self, created in God's way in righteousness and holiness of truth.
>
> Therefore, putting away falsehood, speak the truth, each one to his neighbor, for we are members one of another. Be angry but do not sin; do not let the sun set on your anger, and do not leave room for the devil.... No foul language should come out of your mouths, but only such as is good for needed edification, that it may impart grace to those who hear. (see Ephesians 4)

Sarcasm itself is insensitivity-in-words, but when allowed to take over our speech, our families, our workplaces, our parishes, our schools, and our daily discussions, it injures and poisons the air. Paul wrote that the Gentiles, because of their hardness of heart, had become callous. So it is with sarcasm: it desensitizes us to human suffering and causes us to disregard the injury it inflicts on others. It creates an atmosphere of callous indifference. Christ, to the contrary, calls us to construct his household with words that build up rather than tear down.

A long time ago I made a commitment to myself that when writing or giving a speech I would not use sarcasm or cheap criticism as means of getting a point across. What I have often failed to do is live out that commitment in daily conversation. James and Paul challenge me to be much more vigilant about my casual words and their effect, the means I use to express anger and opinion, and the proper use of my tongue — whose main purpose is to bless God, preach his word, and build up his family in love.

Our Daily Sustenance Comes From God

The performance of the stock market is making folks more than a little nervous. As the value of mutual funds has plummeted, and as other factors have shaken investors' confidence, many have felt the painful consequences. The resulting anxiety is in some ways justified — personal savings have decreased, retirement funds have been devalued or lost, and on and on.

I'm no expert on economics, so I won't offer prognostications or advice. It does seem to me, however, that the market's fragility offers us an opportunity to reflect on a simple yet powerful biblical teaching: Our daily sustenance comes from God.

The first biblical passage to come to mind is the petition "Give us today our daily bread" in the Lord's Prayer. St. Matthew situates Jesus' teaching on prayer in a chapter (6) which also focuses on almsgiving, fasting, heavenly treasure, and anxiety over the things of this life — part of the Sermon on the Mount. Jesus introduces the Lord's Prayer to his disciples ("This is how you are to pray") after having said, "Your Father knows what you need before you ask him."

God is keenly aware of our needs and fulfills them daily. Thus the real question is not whether he will supply them, but whether we ourselves are aware of our true needs, whether we remember that God is their supplier. The petition "Thy will be done on earth as it is in heaven" comes before the petition for our daily bread! The will of God is in a sense our daily bread, for it helps us focus on what we truly need.

It is easy to be filled with anxiety over the stock market, the family, the job, or the future. There is nothing wrong with concern over such things, if it keeps us sharp and on the lookout for wise strategies for the proper care of our families and employees. The danger comes when anxiety levels reach the point where we forget that God is the source of everything, and that our lives are safely in his hands.

Matthew 6 ends with Jesus' admonition, "Do not worry about your life, what you will eat [or drink], or about your body, what you will wear. Is not life more than food and the body more than clothing?" (Matthew 6:25). The birds of the sky can gather nothing for tomorrow's meals, but not to worry — our heavenly Father feeds them. The wildflowers cannot spin thread or cloth, yet our heavenly Father clothes them in robes more splendid than those of Solomon. "If God so clothes the grass of the field, which grows today and is thrown into the oven tomorrow, will he not much more provide for you, O you of little faith?" (Matthew 6:30).

The parable in Matthew 20:1-16 offers a fascinating image to teach the same truth. Workers are hired at various times in one day to work in the landowner's vineyard, yet all receive the same pay, a Roman denarius. In first-century Palestine, this was the customary daily wage. With it, a family could live for a day; without it, they would not be able to meet their basic necessities. When Jesus' landowner pays all the same wage, whether they worked a full sun-scorched day or a mere hour in the afternoon, some grow angry, protesting the inequity.

However, the landowner was generous to all, for all were given their daily sustenance. Had he not gone out of his way to give a daily wage to those who needed it? He had gone to the marketplace five times to offer work to those who needed a day's wages! One of the keys to understanding the parable is that fundamental, yet easy-to-miss, truth: The landowner offered daily sustenance to all. He provided for their needs. So it is with our heavenly Father.

Like everyone else, I hope the market regains strength. I pray that those who have lost life's savings and retirement funds in recent months will recover what was lost. But lately I have often found

Lord, calm any anxiety within me that makes me forget your providential care.

myself reflecting on whether I look trustingly to God for my daily sustenance, daily bread, and daily wage. Did God give me a good start in life, then push me out of the nest to fend for myself? No, says Jesus, everything comes from our heavenly Father, at the beginning and the end of the day. He will never fail to generously provide what I truly need — and more.

Matthew 6 also refers to almsgiving — our sharing with those in need. Since in God's Kingdom earthly treasure is of little value compared to doing God's will, and since everything we own came from his generous hand, the poor have a claim on us. Our care for those in need should be as natural as God's, such that the left hand does not know what the right hand is doing.

"Do not store up for yourselves treasures on earth, where moth and decay destroy, and thieves break in and steal [and markets crash!]. But store up treasures in heaven.... For where your treasure is, there also will your heart be" (Matthew 6:19-21).

Lord, calm any anxiety within me that makes me forget your providential care. Give me a heart that thrives on the daily bread only you can supply.

The Gift of Fear: Fruit of a Filial Love

I once mentioned in a homily the proverb that teaches "the fear of the Lord is the beginning of wisdom." After Mass, several parishioners asked if I would write a column on "fear of the Lord," a concept they found difficult to understand.

Both fear of the Lord and wisdom are important concepts in the Old Testament, and there are a number of places where the sacred authors make a connection between them (e.g., Psalm 111:10, Proverbs 1:7 and 9:10). Isaiah prophesies that after the Babylonian captivity only a stump of David's dynasty will remain, but even from that stump God will bring forth a "shoot," the messianic king:

> But a shoot shall sprout from the stump of Jesse,
> and from his roots a bud shall blossom.
> The spirit of the LORD shall rest upon him:
> a spirit of wisdom and of understanding,
> A spirit of counsel and of strength,
> a spirit of knowledge and of fear of the LORD.
> (Isaiah 11:1-2)

What is fear of the Lord? Does God want us to be afraid of him?

After they had sinned, Adam and Eve "hid themselves from the LORD God among the trees of the garden. The LORD God then called to the man and asked him: 'Where are you?' He answered, 'I heard you in the garden; but I was afraid, because I was naked, so I hid' " (Genesis 3:8-10). Is this fear of the Lord — hiding from God, as if God would harm us? No, not at all.

Jesus tells a parable of the silver pieces entrusted by a man to his servants while he is away. One of the servants dug a hole in the ground and buried his master's money. The servant explained, "Master, I knew you were a demanding person, harvesting where you did not plant and gathering where you did not scatter; so out of fear I went off and buried your talent in the ground" (Matthew 25:24-25). Is that fear of the Lord — paralysis out of fear of doing something wrong? No, not at all.

Fear of the Lord is the Hebrew term for "religion" and means reverence for God.

Fear of the Lord is the Hebrew term for "religion" and means reverence for God. We Christians also understand it as a "gift" of the Holy Spirit, and thus it must be something good for us, not something to make us cower and hide.

At an Angelus address in 1989, St. John Paul II said that fear of the Lord "is a sincere and reverential feeling that a person experiences before the tremendous majesty of God, especially when he reflects upon his own infidelity.... That does not mean an irrational fear, but a sense of responsibility and fidelity to the law."

In other words, fear of the Lord begins with an understanding of God's infinite goodness, boundless omnipotence, and unsurpassed majesty — and his intimate concern for each of us. That wonderful combination gives us much to ponder. As the psalmist wrote:

When I see your heavens, the work of your fingers,
  the moon and stars that you set in place —
What is man that you are mindful of him,
  and a son of man that you care for him?
(Psalm 8:4-5)

This is a mystery to ponder, but it is also a call to live as the One in whose image and likeness we have been created. Jesus' parable about the silver pieces was an invitation to accept his Father's call to be faithful stewards of his limitless generosity.

Fear of the Lord certainly involves an awareness of the justice of God, but it also involves trust in the fatherly concern of God, who wants every person to be saved. The Holy Father continued, "The Holy Spirit instills in the soul most of all a filial love which is a sentiment rooted in the love of God. The soul is now concerned not to displease God whom he loves as a Father, not to offend him in anything, to 'abide in him' and grow in charity."

The Holy Spirit elevates our natural awe of God and God's majesty, and our understanding of sin and its just punishments, and transforms them into a desire, deeply rooted in love (not fear), never to displease God in any way. Perhaps it would be helpful to think of the opposites of fear of the Lord: failure to recognize God's sovereign majesty; lack of regard for God's importance in our lives; lack of reverence; pride in one's own accomplishments while ignoring their ultimate source in God's grace; never attempting to follow God's laws, or treating the teachings of the Bible as just one among many points of view.

As a gift of the Holy Spirit, fear of the Lord is a good and positive thing: When we "delight in the fear of the Lord," we wonder at God's limitless majesty, his intimate love for us, the truth of his law and our responsibility to follow it, and our debt of gratitude and praise to him. To have fear of the Lord is to submit ourselves to God and to be ruled by him in all things. We do not hide out of fear — rather, we run to him, saying with Peter, "Master, to whom shall we go? You have the words of eternal life" (John 6:68).

Offering Encouragement and Sharing the Strength of Christ

A few years ago I wrote a column about Barnabas, an important figure in the Acts of the Apostles. He served as a bridge between disciples of Jesus in the young Church by helping others see how God was active and how his action could be trusted. Barnabas encouraged others to trust in the presence of God — in one another.

Acts tells us that his original name was Joseph. He was a Levite, born in Cyprus. He had sold a piece of property and laid the proceeds at the feet of the apostles. They gave him the name Barnabas, which means "son of encouragement" (see Acts 4:36). It was a fitting name, for that is what Barnabas became to his fellow disciples.

Paul begins the Second Letter to the Corinthians with a brief teaching on true encouragement and its origin in Christ. The passage is worth reflection:

> Blessed be the God and Father of our Lord Jesus Christ, the Father of compassion and God of all encouragement, who encourages us in our every affliction, so that we may be able to encourage those who are in any affliction with the encouragement with which we ourselves are encouraged by God. For as Christ's sufferings overflow to us, so through Christ does our encouragement also overflow. If we are afflicted, it is for your encouragement and salvation; if we are encouraged, it is for your encouragement, which enables you to endure the same sufferings that we suffer. Our hope for you is firm, for we know that as you

share in the sufferings, you also share in the encouragement. (2 Corinthians 1:3-7)

Encouragement is one of the most Christian of deeds.

Paul's understanding of the Church as Christ's body is ever present: he sees that everything comes from Christ, and that all members of the Church share both Christ's sufferings and his consolation. When we suffer, it is Christ who suffers; when we are encouraged, it is Christ's encouragement within us. The bond that believers have with one another because of Christ — the bond Barnabas understood well — is real, tangible, and powerfully present in our lives.

It seems to me that encouragement is one of the most Christian of deeds. Offering encouragement to one another is a way to share the strength that comes from Jesus, a way we make visible the bond that Jesus is between us. It also gives concrete witness to our recognition that we are all in the same boat, and that we are to strengthen and support one another constantly.

In a little treatise titled *Serenity of Heart: Bearing the Troubles of This Life*, St. Francis de Sales comments that "we should behave like people who walk on ice. For these … take each other by the hand or under the arms, so that if one of them slips, the other may hold him up, and that other, when he in his turn is on the point of falling, may be held up by his friend." It's an interesting homespun analogy that illustrates the role we are called to play in one another's lives.

Encouragement is not difficult to offer, and a little goes a long way. We can lift children's spirits by saying "Way to go" when they have accomplished — or almost accomplished — a simple task. Smiles fill their faces, and the smiles translate into confidence the next time they make the attempt. The dynamic is not much different the older we get. Writing a simple note of prayerful support, lending an open ear, overlooking someone's embarrassing blunder, inquiring about the suffering of a family member — these things give heart and strength. Everyone needs a stable hand on the slippery ice.

Just as adults can offer encouragement to little ones, so can little ones encourage their elders, without even knowing it. Smiles, embraces, and a simple "I love you" can make us stand tall with self-assurance and peace. My mother once made an extra birthday cake for one of my nieces, and she told me later that the look of delight on my niece's face made her day.

At times a gesture of encouragement not only makes one's day — it can make one's life. We never know fully what is in another's heart, and our encouragement today might be just what he or she needs to muster courage to take the next step toward a life of peace, fulfillment, and prosperity.

Encouragement also comes in surprising, even challenging forms. I remember several instances when astute advisers gave me just the kick I needed to meet a deadline or fulfill a responsibility. Their encouragement stung, but it was wise and well timed. Likewise, there are times when even those who seem to be working against us can unwittingly provide encouragement by giving us the opportunity to examine the anger or resentment they evoke in us. They can be our teachers, if we humbly look within and ask how we should change.

The source of true, life-changing encouragement is Jesus, whose encouragement we share with one another. With him we can scale any wall, with him we can meet any challenge.

True Wisdom Comes Through a Relationship With Jesus

One Sunday morning many years ago, the priests of my parish had an impromptu discussion in the rectory kitchen about an answer given in the morning paper by a well-known advice columnist. What characterized the column was not only what we believed to be bad advice but also the phrase the columnist appended to it: "And I don't want to hear from any clergymen about this."

Folks seek wisdom from many sources — columnists, books, diets, stars, cards, and just about anything that presents itself as a font of good advice. But who is truly wise? Wisdom is not necessarily the result of great intelligence or years of schooling; some Ph.D.s are not very wise, and some people who have had little formal education possess the wisdom of Solomon. The wisdom called for in raising children can be given a jumpstart by books, but for the most part it is sculpted by the daily experience of parenting, loving, and sacrificing.

Wisdom comes to some people through suffering and to others the moment they refuse to suffer any longer. At times, wisdom is expressed in eloquent words, at other times in silence. It involves knowing certain things and humbly admitting what one does not know. Most of the time genuinely wise people do not realize the depth of their wisdom — and they would never think of hanging out a shingle that reads, "Wisdom To Be Found Here."

True wisdom comes through a relationship with Jesus, one that is fed by prayer. Jesus' parable of the wise and foolish maidens (Matthew 25:1-13) — some of whom brought ample oil for their lamps to keep vigil for the bridegroom, some of whom did not —

is ultimately about keeping the bridegroom (Jesus) always in mind. The wise maidens were wise because they took the bridegroom into consideration in all their plans, even bringing extra oil to keep their lamps burning brightly for him.

The Church celebrates the feast of St. Benedict on July 11 (the Benedictines also celebrate on March 21). Praying the breviary on his feast one summer, I was caught by a response to one of the readings:

> Wishing to please God alone,
> Benedict left his home and patrimony
> to enter the religious life.
>
> — He lived as a hermit in the presence of the all-seeing God.
>
> He withdrew from the world of men,
> knowingly unacquainted with its ways
> and wisely unlearned in its wisdom.

I have often let the phrase roll around in my mind since that summer morning: "knowingly unacquainted with its ways and wisely unlearned in its wisdom." Benedict was no simpleton, nor was he naive about human nature; the rule of life he created for his community has stood the test of time and is known for its keen psychological insight. On his feast, however, the Church remembers not his knowledge but his dependence on God as his only source of wisdom.

No matter how complicated our jobs, our decisions, or our plans; no matter how much education we have received or how capable we are of understanding complex concepts; no matter how much theology we have read or how many words we have written; no matter how many people are in our charge — the task is to keep our hearts simple and to focus simply on Jesus. Father

Jacques Philippe, in *Searching for and Maintaining Peace*, writes: "The certitudes that the habit of prayer inculcates in us are considerably stronger than those that flow from reasoning, even at the highest level of theology."

That is not to say that human wisdom, advice, education, theology, and skills training have no value. To the contrary, they are of immense help, every day. But the Christian places every skill and every bit of knowledge under the light of Jesus, who will lead us straightforwardly, even in darkness, to the place where he wants us. With his guidance, our skills will be used for good, and we will more easily (perhaps even unknowingly) cooperate with what he desires to do.

Our gift of an open heart is all he needs to lead us.

When praying for his guidance, we do not have to come up with a firm "answer" to know that he has heard us. We have to let go of our desire to fix everything and our desire to see results according to our schedule and simply trust that he has accepted our heartfelt desire to do what he wants. Our gift of an open heart is all he needs to lead us.

I find that I worry too much when I place too much trust in myself. Doing my homework, but giving it — abandoning it — all to Jesus, I can rest in the assurance that he has read my heart and will not fail me.

As a bishop, I am of most help to people not when I give them good advice, when I preach a good sermon, or when I write an interesting column — but when I lead them to Jesus. Please God, may it be so.

CHAPTER 3
REMOVING STUMBLING BLOCKS

Jesus Heals Spiritual Blindness

Preparing for a trip to Ecuador some years ago, I decided to read up on this country I had never visited. I discovered many interesting facts and decided to share one with a priest friend. "Hey, did you know that Ecuador is on the equator?" I asked with excitement.

"Hence the name," he responded sarcastically. Those were the days before I began to study Spanish. *Ecuador* is Spanish for "equator." Oh well.

It was another example of a common experience, the kind that makes me blush and laugh with embarrassment: I failed to see something that was as plain as the nose on my face.

A household repair appears complicated but could be easily accomplished. Two things are side-by-side, their connection as clear as a bell, but I fail to see it. The answer to a question eludes me, but I am looking in the wrong place. Something happens in my life that seems to make no sense, but in a matter of weeks it dawns on me that I had been missing a meaning that was there all along. A phrase in the Gospel, a word of Jesus confounds me for years, but in an unexpected instant it makes sense. What took me so long?

I have a feeling that when we get to heaven, in the blink of an eye we will understand a long list of things that had perplexed us in this life — but whose meaning had always been there, as plain as the noses on our faces. We'll blush with embarrassment, and God will smile. He's wanted us to see for a long time.

There's no doubt we will not comprehend everything until we see God face-to-face. But there's also no doubt that in this life faith in Jesus gives us a heart to see and understand many things, and strength to persevere through what we cannot see or understand.

The physically and spiritually blind have always sought him, and of all the Gospel stories about Jesus restoring sight, one particularly appeals to me. First, some context.

Mark's Gospel guides us through the ministry of Jesus, his miracles and his mercy. Jesus calls his disciples, cures demoniacs, restores Peter's mother-in-law to health, cleanses a leper and heals others with many diseases, teaches about the Kingdom, calms a storm at sea, sends the apostles to proclaim the Kingdom, feeds five thousand with five loaves and two fish and four thousand with seven loaves and a few fish, and walks on water in a storm. All these things his disciples had witnessed. But still they did not understand.

Jesus says to them, "Do you not yet understand or comprehend? Are your hearts hardened? Do you have eyes but not see, ears and not hear? … Do you still not understand?" (see Mark 8:14-21).

The phrase "Do you still not understand?" is a kind of turning point in Mark's Gospel, a critical question about the disciples' comprehension of the Kingdom of God. They have followed Jesus and come to know him, but they still do not see all there is to see — they are still afflicted with blindness. Then Jesus performs a miracle which mirrors their situation exactly. They come upon a man who literally had eyes but could not see:

> When they arrived at Bethsaida, they brought to him a blind man and begged him to touch him. He took the blind man by the hand and led him outside the village. Putting spittle on his eyes he laid his hands on him and asked, "Do you see anything?" Looking up he replied, "I see people looking like trees and walking." Then he laid hands on his eyes a second time and he saw clearly; his sight was restored and he could see everything distinctly. (Mark 8:22-25)

We are all blind, at least to some extent, and we miss the nose on our face.

This is an interesting passage because Jesus healed the blind man in stages: At first, people looked to him like walking trees, but after Jesus touched him a second time he could see everything clearly. Like the blind man, the disciples needed repeated contact and growing intimacy with Jesus to see and understand the Kingdom.

I find great comfort in this Gospel story, for at times I, too, am slow to understand even the obvious. I have been a disciple for many years, have seen his love and his grace in action and felt his comfort in trial — yet still I am slow to understand. Following the Lord, seeking to know and love him more, hoping to comprehend all that he wishes me to comprehend, striving to lead the life he wishes me to live, proclaiming a Kingdom I want to know infinitely better myself — I go to Jesus in prayer, asking him to help me see more, see better, and understand. Patiently he leads me, wiping away the fuzziness that stands in the way.

We are all blind, at least to some extent, and we miss the nose on our face. But if we stay close to the Lord Jesus, getting to know him better through prayer and following his way, he will clarify all things in his good time. In the meantime he will lift us up when we stumble. No need for embarrassment — only humility and a desire to follow him.

Transforming Rocks Into Seeds

As I look back through the years, I am much more proud of the seeds I have planted than the rocks I have thrown.

In the late 1950s, our family moved to a new suburb where there were many rocks on yet-unpaved streets — serious temptation for a seven-year-old boy. One afternoon I decided to ride my bike through the neighborhood, and as I did so I collected rocks, occasionally throwing them at enticing targets. Pulling back into our driveway, I realized there was one last rock in my fist. Spying our Rambler station wagon, its rear window cranked down about three inches, I thought to myself, "I can throw this rock through that small opening in the back window."

But I couldn't.

And I didn't.

The poorly thrown rock made contact with the Rambler's safety glass, shattering it into hundreds of small pieces. Using the best and most spontaneous self-defense I could muster, I started crying and ran inside. "What happened?" Mom asked, fearing the worst. "The window broke," I tearfully replied.

After some fancy verbal footwork — I was going too fast on my bike and ran into the back of the car and my hand hit the window and it broke and no I'm not bleeding and I didn't know the glass could break and I can sweep it up — I succeeded in convincing Mom that it had been a freak accident and that I was lucky to have survived unscathed.

Or so I thought.

One afternoon a couple of years ago, sitting with Mom at the kitchen table, I heard her ask out of the blue, "Peter, do you remember the time the back windshield of the Rambler broke?"

Though by then she was in her eighties and I was in my fifties, I felt the old fear creep up my back. Of course she knew. She had known all along.

A few years after the rock incident, my best friend Larry and I decided to plant a garden in my backyard. With the fervor of cotton farmers, but without their skill, we dug out an eight-by-twelve section of the yard and planted carrots, mustard greens, green beans, and lettuce. Within days, the seeds had sprouted, and within weeks there was food on the table. But soon we tired of garden tending, weeds overtook the plot, and my dog slept in the cool greens.

Much to my amazement, however, the vegetables kept growing all season, despite the weeds, the dog, and our neglect. There was fresh produce for months, hearty survivors of the short-lived summer project of two bored adolescents. Even today I suspect there may be an eight-by-twelve depression in the backyard of 3939 Graceland Drive in Memphis.

The scribes and Pharisees once dragged before Jesus a woman caught in adultery, hoping to embarrass him and caring little about her. Rocks in hand, they were ready to execute her for the crime. "Let the one among you who is without sin be the first to throw a stone at her," said Jesus. One by one, rocks dropped from guilty hands, their audible thuds stirring up swirls of dust. The elders backed away first, fleeing their own embarrassment. Jesus said to the terrified woman, "Where are they? Has no one condemned you?" "No one, sir," she replied. "Neither do I condemn you," said Jesus. "Go, [and] from now on, do not sin any more" (see John 8:1-11).

Jesus once told a parable about a farmer who went out to sow seeds. Since in those days sowing often preceded plowing, much seed was wasted. Some fell on the path, where birds came and feasted; some fell on rocky ground, where it had little soil and scorched in the sun; some fell among thorns, which choked it. But some fell on rich soil, where it produced beyond all expectation. The seed is God's word, said Jesus, and though in the sowing it often falls on unsuitable ground and sprouts for just a while, it will nonetheless eventually yield a rich harvest — because God is the sower, and his seed does his work. When the earth is plowed and ready — when a human heart is humble and receptive — the joy of the harvest is great.

We can ask God to transform those stones into seeds, his seeds.

Through the years I have thrown rocks, and I have planted seeds. The rock throwing is a source of embarrassment and sadness, but the seed sowing is a source of humble satisfaction. Whether the rocks were literal, verbal, or attitudinal, they did no one any good and often caused harm. Whether the seeds were literal, spiritual, or pastoral, if they had their origin in God they somehow did his work.

Perhaps at times I didn't tend the Lord's field as lovingly as I could or gave in to fatigue or frustration, and perhaps at times his seed fell where it was not welcome. Perhaps I self-righteously wanted to claim the yield as my own or moved on before harvest and never saw the yield with my own eyes. Nonetheless, I can trust that the seed did its work — that God did his work — and that according to his plan I played a small part in building the Kingdom.

When our knuckles are white from fists clinched tight, holding stones in the ready position, we can ask God to transform those stones into seeds, his seeds. Where we might have caused harm, he will bring life.

Examining Myself in Light of My Pet Peeves

When I'm in a hurry, I always seem to break a shoelace tying my shoes. Won't buy that brand of shoelace again.

When I'm late for an appointment, I always seem to make myself even later by trying a shortcut. Why are these darn streets so poorly marked?

When I'm in a strange city, it always seems that other people drive like maniacs. Why don't they drive like me?

When I'm frustrated with myself, I seem to be most apt to say a cross word to someone else. What's wrong with these people?

Certain circumstances draw out the worst in me, though my initial reaction is to point the blame elsewhere. That's usually the way it works with pet peeves.

Pet peeves raise my ire, get my dander up, make me clench my fists or throw up my hands in frustration. They are those annoying imperfections I observe in the world around me, which in my estimation just shouldn't be there. Often my pet peeves have to do with things that keep happening, or people who keep behaving the same way, even though I have already expressed my disagreement. My pet peeves can even cause me to give an impromptu lecture on what I learned in school. An early morning pet peeve can ruin a whole day.

I have my share of pet peeves, but in the scheme of things they are unimportant and probably useless to those around me. They are knee-jerk judgments I render on people and the world based on perspectives to which I tenaciously, though often uncritically, cling. My pet peeves can cause me to expend lots of emotional energy, often in spurts. I have learned from observing how I let them affect me that when I insist on everyone else being reasonable as I define "reasonable," I become the most unreasonable of all.

There is a difference between having righteous anger over something that is clearly wrong, immoral, false, or harmful, and having a pet peeve. For example, we have a responsibility to defend our faith when it is being taught falsely; we have a duty to defend someone whose rights are being denied; it can be an act of justice and charity to confront another about a serious fault that has affected us or others. If we never act on righteous anger, we give the impression that anything goes. Acting on pet peeves, however, creates its own set of problems.

Pet peeves aren't problematic because they're totally wrong, for they might well contain some measure of validity. They are problematic because, for the most part, they are about me. I take something potentially important and reduce its importance to how it affects me. Pet peeves seem to be about how the world "out there" should change, but for the most part they're about how I should change.

It helps to take a look at pet peeves and ask why I clutch them so tightly. Many times I discover that the reason I had let myself be bothered by them was that there was something going on in my life (I was hurried, late, worried, hurt) which needed attention, and I let my frustration with myself color my attitude. To my embarrassment, I notice that I am often guilty of the very subject of my pet peeve. I hear the voice of St. Paul: "You are without excuse, every one of you who passes judgment. For by the standard by which you judge another you condemn yourself, since you, the judge, do the very same things" (Romans 2:1).

Most of us would be more peace-filled throughout the day — as would those around us — if, when our pet peeves grab hold of us, we drop them, then and there, with a laugh. "There I go again."

When it comes to morality, Jesus says clearly that wrong is wrong and evil is evil. But when it comes to judgment, I should begin with myself.

"Stop judging, that you may not be judged. For as you judge, so will you be judged, and the measure with which you measure will be measured out to you. Why do you notice the splinter in your brother's eye, but do not perceive the wooden beam in your own eye?" (see Matthew 7:1-5)

When it comes to judgment, I should begin with myself.

"The measure with which you measure will be measured out to you." I am reminded of a retreat director who once said, "Life gives us change back in the currency with which we do business." He meant that the reactions we elicit from others often spring from the way we have approached them in the first place. Have I scowled or been demanding or sarcastic? Have I packed so many expectations into an hour that I have rushed around frantically, stretching to the breaking point not only my shoelaces but also my patience? Is it possible that my pet peeves would not have been ruffled had I behaved more considerately in the first place, or had I been on time and not in a hurry?

Paul encouraged the Romans (14:13), "Then let us no longer judge one another, but rather resolve never to put a stumbling block or hindrance in the way of a brother." Perhaps a good antidote to the power pet peeves have over us is to take a good look at ourselves, then pave a smooth road for those around us with kindness, patience, forgiveness, and humility.

God's Love Brings Order to Our Souls

One hot afternoon two thousand years ago, some locals came upon a water jar abandoned next to a well in the town of Sychar. I wonder if they inquired of their neighbors if anyone knew who owned it, or if they simply looked quickly in both directions before picking it up to take home as their own. No matter. The previous owner had no further use for it.

Until just a few hours earlier, it had belonged to a nameless Samaritan woman whose encounter with Jesus is reported in the fourth chapter of John. She had gone to the well at noon, the jar slung lazily under her arm, to draw water from the public cistern. No one was around at the hour when folks went home to eat and rest, and she liked it that way. To the locals she was well known, the kind of person they whispered and joked about, someone stuck in the cistern of her disappointments with no way out. At that hour, she could fill her jar in peace.

But on this day when the woman came to draw water, Jesus was resting by the well after a tiring journey from Judea. Smarting from five failed marriages and the derision of the townspeople, she was suspicious of the likes of him. But by his patience, his humor, his prophetic knowledge — his love — he gradually brought her to faith. John wants us to notice that this happened at noon, when the sun was straight up in the sky and shone straight down to the depths of Jacob's well — and the depths of the woman's bitterness. For the first time, she could see things clearly because Jesus enlightened her gloom.

Having recognized who he was, having been given a way out of the hole she had dug for herself, she went into town to tell folks all about it. In her haste, she left the jar behind.

Most of us know what it is like to be a stagnant cistern.

There must have been something different about her appearance as she talked about Jesus, else they would have paid her no mind. Perhaps it was the look of freedom and peace, the look of someone unburdened and unstuck, the look of someone whose thirst was finally quenched.

Most of us know what it is like to be a stagnant cistern, at least during certain periods of our lives, just as we know what it is like to ache for loved ones who feel stuck with no way out. At those times, we let wounds inflicted long ago fester within, we won't talk out our troubles, we distrust the lives and intentions of others (even those who love us most), we lug around the burden of sin without seeking forgiveness. It is to us at those times that Jesus comes to pour out his water of life, to shine his light of peace.

Recognizing that everything in the Samaritan woman's life was out of place and out of sorts, Jesus by his love brought order to her — his Father's order, the order for which she had been created in the first place. That's what God's love does: It brings order to our souls.

A priest friend once told me that, and recently I asked him to explain further. He said he gained the insight from the life of St. Francis of Assisi:

> In my time as a priest working in Hispanic ministry, I have always had people tell me that I give *buen consejos* ("good advice"). I always knew that I wasn't saying anything profound, but whatever I said seemed to help. Francis let me know that it wasn't so much the words I was saying but the intense love that I was feeling for the people who were in front of me. That love is what was ordering their souls, and they began to understand,

> or rather what was causing them to have problems was changed within them. It is a gift to have this, and this is what Francis was able to do with people.

My friend does have that gift: It is the gift of loving others with the love of Jesus. It is Jesus who — by his life, death, and resurrection — restored order to creation, and it is he who restores order to our souls when they have been shattered to pieces.

Jesus invites us both to drink from his love and to love others, particularly those stuck in their own cisterns, through him. It is not so much what we say or what we do, but that we desire to love them with his love. Patiently, kindly, persistently, mercifully, he will restore order to their souls, just as he did for the woman of Samaria.

More than four centuries ago, facing troubles enough to discourage anyone and meeting roadblocks at every turn, St. John of the Cross did not succumb to cynicism. Rather, he wrote that "where there is no love, put love, and there you will draw out love."

The Samaritan woman had gone to Jacob's well at noon to draw water, but she rushed away after meeting Jesus, leaving her jar behind. It was he who had given her to drink, who drew out of her the love his Father had placed within her the moment she was conceived. So will he do for you and for me.

Speaking the Truth in Love

I have noticed that election season demonstrates an unflattering characteristic of twenty-first-century America: our tendency to quarrel and accuse rather than rationally consider the issues at hand. Sound bites seem to carry more weight than moral principles. The way we engage in political debate polarizes rather than unites.

But enough about politics. I would like to consider what Scripture teaches about how we interact with one another at every level. Behavior we notice in the political arena offers a backdrop for examining how we give witness to our faith, whether the topic is terrorism, religion, or the price of gas.

We have many opportunities to give witness to our faith. We are often questioned about Catholic beliefs and challenged to explain their validity, and perhaps at times we are tempted to react with emotion rather than faith. In discussions with friends and coworkers about any number of non-religious topics, we come face-to-face with the tendency to draw up sides, choose corners, and polarize.

In the first of his letters, Peter invites Christians to understand the nature of our community and how God calls us to interact with one another. He encourages us to live in a way consistent with our new life and proposes obedience, reverence, and mutual love. Those being built into God's spiritual house, he writes, reject malice, deceit, insincerity, envy, and slander. They give good example to non-believers, are good citizens, follow the humble example of Jesus, and live in unity with one another.

He concludes this section with an intriguing word of encouragement in a time of hostility: "Always be ready to give an explanation to anyone who asks you for a reason for your hope, but do it with gentleness and reverence, keeping your conscience clear, so that, when you are maligned, those who defame your good conduct in Christ may themselves be put to shame" (1 Peter 3:15-16).

We can be maligned (or feel maligned) for a variety of reasons and in a variety of ways. The question is: How will we respond?

We can be maligned (or feel maligned) for a variety of reasons and in a variety of ways. The question is: How will we respond?

Peter suggests we respond with hope-filled gentleness and reverence for the other person, so that while speaking the truth we will also be imitating our humble Savior. Did Jesus verbally assault opponents with clever arguments in order to embarrass them? Did he summarily condemn people who were in error, or did he patiently lead them to the right path? A sarcastic comeback may grab a few laughs or give a momentary sense of satisfaction, but we have failed if we have not spoken the truth while imitating our Lord.

Peter was writing about how we communicate the hope that is in us because of Christ. His premise was that there is such a thing as truth, and it is found fully in Christ. Christians are to live the truth; thus, when a Christian speaks about it, others may see that he or she is also putting it into practice. We are filled with hope, even at times of hostility, precisely because Christ, the Truth, speaks for himself. He has no need of our clever arguments, our sarcasm, or our angry debate. Rather, he asks that we become shining examples of his truth.

In the coming months, we will watch many debates, hear many insults, and be asked our opinions (and that's not even considering the presidential election!). In certain circumstances, we may be tempted to speak and react in un-Christian ways. We will infuse the peace of Christ into our homes, our workplaces, and this season of political heat if we remember the counsel of Peter and always speak the truth in love, as did our Lord.

God Accepts Us Even in Our Humiliations

Arriving at my office one morning years ago, I noticed that the orange tag from the dry cleaners was still attached to the end of my suit coat. I reached down and yanked it off with an embarrassed smile. I would have thought nothing of it, and there would have been no embarrassment, had I not just finished recording a video message for a diocesan program and then given a talk to thirty-five women making a Cursillo weekend. The women were kind enough not to mention the bright orange tag at the end of my sleeve — and as for the men who recorded the video message, well, I doubt they noticed.

Vesting in the sacristy before a diaconate ordination one morning, I found a sheet of fabric softener stuck to the Velcro fastener on my alb. Luckily, I pulled it free before putting on my chasuble and prevented the sheet from falling to the floor during Mass.

At the start of an early-morning philosophy class many years ago, Father Timothy announced he would not count a certain question from a recent pop quiz because it had not been part of that day's reading assignment. I raised my hand and asked with interest, "Father Timothy, what was the answer to that question?" With a "gotcha" kind of smile, he responded: "If you had read last night's assignment, you would know the answer."

Those weren't the first times I have embarrassed myself, and they certainly won't be the last. But I always find it interesting to observe my own reaction when I have done or said something foolish. I pretend nothing happened, or that I meant to make a fool of myself; I give in to the knee-jerk need to defend myself, to everyone's further amusement; I am annoyed by the laughter I have caused; I am angry at myself; I laugh with everyone else, painfully aware that my foolish mistake has been exposed.

All of which is good for my humility.

God is neither embarrassed nor self-conscious about associating with us.

If I am truly paying attention at such times, I will learn from my reactions and my embarrassment — not so that I will never embarrass myself again, for I will surely do that, but so that I will come to terms with the fact that sometimes I take myself too seriously. Such experiences can help purify my motives, lessen my pride, and make me more compassionate.

Our minor embarrassments pale in comparison to those times we fail utterly, when we disappoint ourselves and others, or when by the prideful stubbornness of our self-will or the sheer meanness of someone who does not like us we are completely humiliated. Our reactions at such times can vary greatly, with overwhelming intensity. It is important never to give in to discouragement, because it can cause us to stray off the path that leads to God.

A little reflection when we are embarrassed or humiliated can take us even beyond a better understanding of ourselves to a deeper understanding of God and the unselfconsciousness of his love. Whether our foolishness has been exposed by a minor embarrassment or we have been utterly humiliated and cast down, if we look up to God in prayer, we will see him nodding, prodding, and encouraging us to stand up again. In his Son, he knows what it means to face humiliation. On the cross, he bore the total, raw weight of our most profound failures, sins, vexations, and humiliations — because we could not bear it ourselves.

God is neither embarrassed nor self-conscious about associating with us, our foolishness and failures notwithstanding. Love is not wrenched from him begrudgingly, stretched by us to its limits but elastic enough to keep us in his care. It is an extraordinary truth that God loves us so much that he did not hesitate to take on our human nature. Nothing is stolen from him — he gives himself freely and deliberately. That's how God is. "This is why the Father loves me, because I lay down my life in order to take it up again. No one takes it from me, but I lay it down on my own" (John 10:17-18).

In Letter 232, addressed to the people of Madaura, St. Augustine wrote:

> Therefore the Christ who is preached throughout the whole world is not Christ adorned with an earthly crown, nor Christ rich in earthly treasures, nor Christ illustrious for earthly prosperity, but Christ crucified. This was ridiculed, at first, by whole nations of proud men, and is still ridiculed by a remnant among the nations; but it was the object of faith at first to a few and now to whole nations, because when Christ crucified was preached at that time, notwithstanding the ridicule of the nations, to the few who believed, the lame received power to walk, the dumb to speak, the deaf to hear, the blind to see, and the dead were restored to life. Thus, at length, the pride of this world was convinced that, even among the things of this world, there is nothing more powerful than the humility of God.

When life demonstrates to me — when I demonstrate to myself — how limited and foolish I can be and how easily embarrassed or humiliated, it is God's humility that reminds me again of his unsurpassed love. And it is his love that refines me, like gold and silver are refined, burning my self-consciousness and pretense like so much dross.

Removing the Risk: Giving Our Hearts to What Satisfies

On a rural highway in north-central Arkansas, there is an abandoned building, ramshackle and weed-covered after years of neglect, which once housed a local business. Driving down the highway, one cannot help but notice the building, because painted on its roof is the name of its former occupant: "Risky's Security Storage."

I'm sure Risky was a fine person, and I hope the closing of his business did not cause him financial ruin, but I could not help but smile at the name. I'm just not sure I would want to leave my valuables at a place called "Risky's."

The incongruity of the name was so obvious that it immediately caught my attention. But it also got me to thinking about ironies — even contradictions — in my own life which may be subtle but are equally telling. Are there areas in which I say one thing but unwittingly do another? Do I tell myself that my intentions and goals are set solidly in one direction but put them in jeopardy by following another, risky path? Do I leave some habits completely unexamined and idly allow myself to be lulled in a direction opposite my deepest aspirations, dragged down by the feet even as I climb the Lord's mountain?

Hypocrisy can be glaring and deliberate, a kind of posturing and pretending intended to advance ourselves or appear better than we are. But it can also be subtle, unwitting and unintended, unclear to us but obvious to others. Witting or unwitting, such inconsistencies deserve our attention. Left unexamined, they can eventually lead us off course, far from our goals and opposed to our greatest needs.

In *Together on the Road: A Vision of Lived Communion for the Church and the Priesthood*, Father Massimo Camisasca writes:

> Anyone who knows how to man a sailboat on high seas knows how important the tiniest of corrections can be when the winds and currents multiply effects to infinity. Life is like this, too: a small correction can have infinite repercussions on our existence.

It is not that every fault is equally serious, every sin equally weighty, or every correction equally urgent. Moreover, we need not be anxious that habitual venial sins will cause our eternal damnation. But it is quite possible that out of neglect, ignorance, or laziness we altogether ignore the need to work on minor faults, assuming that because they are minor they are of no consequence. As Father Camisasca indicates, small course corrections can make a big difference.

The literal meaning of the Greek word for sin is "to miss the mark" — to fail to attain the goal.

It is interesting to note that the literal meaning of the Greek word for sin is "to miss the mark" — to fail to attain the goal. Life is full of course corrections, and only with God's grace do we notice and admit the need and then follow through with corrective action. Conversion is a lifelong project.

The Catholic tradition of examining one's conscience is very helpful in this regard. Prayerfully examining our behavior in light of the Ten Commandments, the Gospels, the Beatitudes, Church teaching, and the Golden Rule, we receive insight into the incongruities, inconsistencies, contradictions — and riskiness — of the patterns into which we have settled. A good examination of conscience requires seriousness and humor, honesty and humility. On the one hand, we learn to laugh at our frailty and not take ourselves too seriously — "Lord, there I go again!" On the other hand, we learn to admit in humility that something needs to be done — "Lord, help me not go there again!" Most of all, we learn how much we need God's help and how eager he is to provide it.

Years ago I found a simple bit of wisdom (and a helpful tool for examining my conscience) in a saying of one of the Desert Fathers (solitary monks and nuns of the fourth and fifth centuries). Abba Poeman, "the Shepherd," once said, "Do not give your heart to that which does not satisfy your heart."

I can fritter away my time, my energy, my attention, my money, my affections — my heart — by feeding myself things which are not good for me. A big, gooey cinnamon roll may taste delicious with the morning coffee, but it cannot supply the nutrients I need to meet the tasks of the morning. In the same way, it is possible to "feed" myself with all manner of entertainment, conversation, and preoccupation, none of which can nourish me — and much of which can ultimately harm me.

The flip side of Abba Poeman's advice is equally helpful: Give your heart to that which satisfies your heart.

God, faith, family, sacred Scripture, the Eucharist and other sacraments, prayer, good reading, humility, love, mercy, contrition, generosity, sacrifice, truth — these are the things that truly nourish our hearts, help us correct our course, resolve every incongruity and inconsistency, keep us from putting ourselves at risk, and set us solidly on course, straight as an arrow toward fulfillment in God.

Letting Go of Grudges

I once asked a group of grade-schoolers, "What's a grudge?" Only one hand went up, that of eight-year-old Kelly, an only child from a broken home.

"It's when you hold all the madness inside," she said.

Kelly's response was perfect, and for a moment I was speechless. I knew her to be a little girl who held no grudges, though she probably had good reason to do so. I smiled and thanked her for such an insightful answer. I have often quoted her.

Grudges weigh us down, keep us tight-fisted and tense, turn us inside out, and make us wince when someone even lightly touches our emotions, much as we do when there is an open sore on the skin. Holding tight to grudges, we allow ourselves to be fooled into thinking we somehow control the one who harmed us by clinging to our madness and anger. Grudges are a kind of solitary, sometimes secret, revenge. But the one being harmed the most is the one who holds the grudge.

There was no bitterness in Jesus, though some people deliberately derided and ridiculed him. He held no grudges, though some people intentionally harmed him. He had no desire for vengeance, though some accused him of crimes they themselves had committed. In Jesus there was only patience for the sinner, and mercy.

In the *Mirror of Love*, St. Aelred once wrote that the perfection of brotherly love is found in Jesus' love for those who harmed him, particularly his forgiveness of his executioners. Aelred recalls the image of the Suffering Servant in Isaiah:

> Though harshly treated, he submitted
> and did not open his mouth;

> Like a lamb led to slaughter
> or a sheep silent before shearers,
> he did not open his mouth. (Isaiah 53:7)

With novel insight into the mercy of Jesus, Aelred writes:

> It was not enough to pray for them [his executioners]: he wanted also to make excuses for them. "Father, forgive them, for they do not know what they are doing." They are great sinners, yes, but they have little judgment; therefore, "Father, forgive them." They are nailing me to the cross, but they do not know who it is that they are nailing to the cross: "if they had known, they would never have crucified the Lord of glory; therefore, Father, forgive them."
>
> They think I am a lawbreaker, an imposter claiming to be God, a seducer of the people. I have hidden my face from them, and they do not recognize my glory; therefore, "Father, forgive them, for they do not know what they are doing."

Aelred was not implying that Jesus was ignorant of the intentions of those who harmed him, that he was naive to the power of evil, or that we should gloss over the damage inflicted by the devil on the world around us. To the contrary, like Isaiah he presents Jesus as one who consciously, deliberately, and intentionally bore the weight of our sin and the chaos caused by Satan's evil strategies. Jesus was fully aware of everything that brought about his suffering — more aware than any of us can be when we suffer — and breaking through the human cycle of grudge and revenge, he forgave.

When we see Jesus on the cross, the effects and ramifications of our sin are before us in stark relief — but so are the release and freedom won by his perfect love. Jesus will always be our expert advocate — "Father, forgive them" — because he bore our sin in all its ugliness and is the only one qualified to speak on our behalf. If anyone has the "right" to hold a grudge, it is Jesus. But he does not: his love burns up our sin in one everlasting sacrifice, as fire refines gold or silver by burning off the dross.

If anyone has the "right" to hold a grudge, it is Jesus. But he does not.

Living in Christ means letting go of grudges, forsaking vengeful attitudes and words, letting out all the "madness" by forgiving those who have harmed us. It is difficult to forgive, and we might have to begin by asking God to give us the desire to forgive. Step by step he will show us the folly of our tight fists and open sores and instill in us the will to let go of anger and revenge. He will remind us to look to the cross and see how his Son wiped up the mess of our sin, carried it away on the cross, and burned it up in love.

I find it helpful to picture the rock-carrying elders who dragged the adulterous woman before Jesus to be "tried" for her sin. It was Jesus who was on trial, of course. When he invited any elder without sin to cast a stone at the woman, one by one they left him, rocks dropping to the ground. You can almost hear the thuds and see the dust swirl up as they fall.

If we find it hard to drop the stone of grudges, we can at least begin by handing them to Jesus, who will gently place them on the ground before us. Freed of the extra weight, we will be on the road to forgiveness.

Simple Steps to Growth in God's Friendship

How does one strive to know the Lord? How does one become God's intimate friend? Perhaps these simple points will help:

Speak to God. Carrying on a conversation with God in prayer, the same kind I have with close friends, gives me the chance to tell him what's in my heart and on my mind. As in all friendships, honesty is required. Why lie to God?

Listen to God. Prayer is much more than getting things off my chest. It also involves quietly giving God the opportunity to respond. As St. John of the Cross once remarked, God speaks his everlasting word in silence. In our noisy world, we must not forget that silence can be much more intimate than speech.

Read what God has to say. This is another way of saying, "Read the Bible." The Bible recounts what God has revealed to us about himself through creation, history, prophecy, and most especially through the Son, his perfect self-revelation. And as Rabbi Abraham Heschel once wrote, the Bible is also God's book about man. We learn both about God and about ourselves by opening the sacred Scriptures.

Learn the faith. Faith has an objective component: the truths we are to believe. By studying the Church's teaching, we give heart *and* mind to God.

Become true disciples of God's Son. The Father sent the Son so that we could abide in the deep intimacy they share. "Father, they are your gift to me.... I made known to them your name and I will make it known, that the love with which you loved me may be in them and I in them." (John 17:24, 26). Jesus is the Way, and giving our lives in discipleship takes us to the bosom of the Father.

Commit yourself to a life of conversion. Being a disciple of the Lord Jesus involves allowing his grace to go to work in me — to transform me more and more into Christ himself. This is entirely the work of grace, but God calls me to cooperate with grace. Do not grieve the Holy Spirit! I am called to discover my sinfulness and repent. I am called to accept the gift of God's merciful forgiveness. I am called to change what needs to be changed in my life. I am called to do good and avoid evil, to relinquish habits and ways of living which are not compatible with faith in Christ and thus not compatible with Christ's living presence in me. The goal is to say — and to live! — with St. Paul: "For to me life is Christ" (Philippians 1:21).

Being a disciple of the Lord Jesus involves allowing his grace to go to work in me.

Make of yourself a living sacrifice. "I urge you therefore, brothers, by the mercies of God, to offer your bodies as a living sacrifice, holy and pleasing to God, your spiritual worship. Do not conform yourselves to this age but be transformed by the renewal of your mind, that you may discern what is the will of God, what is good and pleasing and perfect" (Romans 12:1-2).

Learn to be humble. Humility means not only that I seek to be of loving service to others and tend to their needs; it also means that I develop a constant awareness that everything I have, everything I am, is God's gift. Therefore, "Whoever boasts, should boast in the Lord" (2 Corinthians 10:17). Humility also means that I lovingly and trustingly give myself over to the law of God, who knows what is best for me; and even when I do not understand his ways, I offer myself to him in humble obedience, that he may form me according to his ways.

Learn who is greatest in the Kingdom of God. Jesus makes clear that "little ones" have priority in his Kingdom: children, the poor, the sick, the imprisoned, "widows and orphans."

Call on the Holy Spirit. From the beginning to the end of time, whenever the Father sends the Son, he also sends the Spirit, because their mission is inseparable. The Spirit keeps us faithful and makes intimacy with God possible.

Seek out the presence and action of God. The sacraments are the public worship of the Church, but they are first and foremost the work of Christ. If we want to know God better, we look for opportunities to be where he is at work, especially the sacraments of Eucharist and Penance.

Love the Mother of God. As the first disciple, the Blessed Mother gives us the best example of giving oneself to God, and she is our powerful intercessor. She presents our need to Jesus ("They have no wine") and directs us to him ("Do whatever he tells you"; see John 2:1-11).

Make friends with the friends of God. Reading the lives and writings of the saints reminds us that we are surrounded by great witnesses who inspire us to live faith to the full. Likewise, surrounding ourselves in daily life with friends who share our love for God helps us stay the course.

"Do not give your heart to that which does not satisfy your heart," wrote Abba Poeman. Poeman was referring to the fact that we often amuse ourselves and spend our time with things — entertainments, conversations, etc. — which can never nourish us because we were made for greater things. That which seems harmless on the surface can gradually erode the quality and depth of our commitment to the Lord.

Letter to a Friend on Forgiveness

I would like to write to you who fear you are not worthy of God's forgiveness.

Dear Friend,

For reasons known perhaps only to you, you have decided you are unworthy of God's mercy. You have been on my mind lately, and in recent days I have felt strongly that God was nudging me to write a few words of hope to you. Do not be afraid! You are the very one Jesus is looking for so that he may tell you, "Your sins are forgiven."

It is not uncommon for folks to come to a turning point in life, one brought about by a particular event, the look of hurt on another's face, the birth of a child, or the sheer passing of years, a turning point at which they say to themselves, "I have done wrong, and I must live my life differently from now on."

They begin to ask worrisome questions: "Will God forgive me? I do not deserve his love. I have wasted so many years. Is it too late for me to start again? Will God look askance at me, wondering if I am really serious? What about those I hurt? Will they ever forgive me? How can I make it up to them? What if I fall again? Am I a hypocrite for seeking forgiveness?"

If you are one of these, I say to you again: Do not be afraid! You are the very one Jesus is looking for so that he may tell you, "Your sins are forgiven."

Regret, shame, embarrassment, and sorrow are powerful human emotions unleashed when we come to the realization that we have done wrong and that our wrongdoing has affected others. Such emotions can be very helpful — even agents of healing — if we expose them to the light of God's love. But they can also do us damage if we allow ourselves to be paralyzed by them or if we think we are doomed to flounder in them for the rest of our lives.

Jesus' attention was always focused on those paralyzed by the burdens of life — sinners, the sick, the weak in faith, the fearful and hopeless. He himself said it was to these — the "lost" — that the Father had sent him. Think of it this way: If you were one of those in the many crowds through which Jesus passed during his public ministry, he would have noticed you. He would have sought you out.

You may wonder: "Would he have noticed me because guilt was written all over my face, because I was ugly compared to the others whose faith seemed strong and who had lived much better lives than I? Would he have wondered why I was among such a group of good people? Would he have said to me, 'Come back when you are clean, when your house is in perfect order?' "

Why would Jesus have sought you out? Because he loves you. Because you need him. Because he wants you to accept his gift of forgiveness. Because he wants you with him eternally.

Read the seventh and eighth chapters of St. Paul's Letter to the Romans. Paul writes very personally, even a little painfully, of his frustration with himself: "What I do, I do not understand. For I do not do what I want, but I do what I hate" (7:15). One can sense the confusion he has experienced as his sinfulness has been exposed to him: "Miserable one that I am! Who will deliver me from this mortal body? Thanks be to God through Jesus Christ our Lord" (7:24-25).

God had given Paul the insight that he had been rescued from sin by God's free and undeserved gift of grace in Jesus. Once a fierce persecutor of Christians, he now preached the Gospel he once rejected, proclaiming that all of us without exception are the objects of God's redeeming, rescuing, ransoming, re-creating mercy. That means you.

The very fact that you are aware of your sin and want to change is a sign that God is already at work in you. Tell him you are sorry. Place yourself in his arms. Trust in his mercy. God's mercy is a gift — we cannot earn it. None of us deserves it, but he forgives us nonetheless. God sent his Son to look for the lost and bring them back. He aches for you to be at peace in his household. Look into his face and see not hurt but mercy.

Tell him you are sorry.
Place yourself in his arms.
Trust in his mercy.

Yes, perhaps some changes will be needed in your life. Jesus' gift of forgiveness was accompanied by his challenge to "sin no more." Perhaps you will fall again. But it is much better to hand over your weakness to God having realized your sin and his mercy than to stand apart from the crowd, fearing from afar that you are not one of those for whom he is looking. It is better to let God be your strength than to think you can be strong on your own.

These few words are only a part of what I would like to say to you. Go to your pastor and tell him you are seeking God's forgiveness. Go to confession, if you have not already done so. Unburden your heart and let him tell you the rest of the story of God's love.

And don't forget: You are the very one Jesus is looking for so that he may tell you, "Your sins are forgiven." Be at peace. It is never too late to start again. You can live the rest of your life in thanksgiving.

Your friend in Christ,
Archbishop Sartain

CHAPTER 4
ENCOUNTERING GOD IN PRAYER

Allowing God to Teach Us to Pray

Like Abraham (Genesis 18), we all do our share of bargaining with God. Like Jacob (Genesis 32), we do our share of wrestling with God. Like Jonah (Jonah 1), we do our share of running from God. Like Peter (Matthew 26, Mark 14, Luke 22), we do our share of denying God. And like Thomas (John 20) we do our share of doubting him.

At times, we are quite conscious of bargaining, wrestling, running, denying, or doubting; a day of distraction or a night of tossing and turning might be the result. But at other times, we engage in these exercises without giving them a second thought, as a flood of words or thoughts streams through our minds when we pray. This is our way of trying to figure things out (or avoid figuring them out) in the presence of God. It's the most natural thing in the world, and needless to say, God is used to it.

For example, it's natural for us to offer a solution to God when facing a dilemma. "If only you will do such-and-such, God, things will be okay." Afflicted by what he called a "thorn in the flesh," St. Paul prayed for resolution: "That I might not become too elated, a thorn in the flesh was given to me, an angel of Satan, to beat me, to keep me from being too elated. Three times I begged the Lord about this, that it might leave me" (2 Corinthians 12:7-8).

Paul did not reveal the nature of his painful thorn, but he wanted to be rid of it, and he prayed to that end. The answer God gave was surprising: "He said to me, 'My grace is sufficient for you, for power is made perfect in weakness' " (2 Corinthians 12:9). The thorn was not to be taken away, and Paul learned a powerful lesson: that God's grace reveals its power and beauty when we humbly receive him in utter weakness. Paul might never have learned this lesson — to the contrary, he might have persisted in the illusion of his own strength — had God not allowed this jab at his pride.

Our inability to pray as we ought is not cause for discouragement.

Perhaps building on this experience, Paul also wrote that we do not know how to pray as we ought (Romans 8:26). In his case, he had prayed for the removal of a thorn that God knew would be helpful to him. At times, we pray for things we wrongfully judge to be good for us when in fact they would not be; we pray for only a little when God wants to give us a lot; we pray for a quick fix when God wants to heal us.

Our inability to pray as we ought is not cause for discouragement. In a sense, it is another helpful thorn in the flesh. Paul writes:

> In the same way, the Spirit too comes to the aid of our weakness; for we do not know how to pray as we ought, but the Spirit itself intercedes with inexpressible groanings. And the one who searches hearts knows what is the intention of the Spirit, because it intercedes for the holy ones according to God's will. (Romans 8:26-27)

There is no reason to fear when we seem to hit a roadblock in prayer, for the Spirit intercedes on our behalf. Our sight is conditioned by what we know and experience, but the Holy Spirit knows and sees all things with eternal clarity. He prays in us and for us, that we might grow in our desire for what is truly right for us and for those for whom we pray. The Spirit "intercedes for the holy ones according to God's will."

In a letter to Proba, St. Augustine wrote:

> Therefore, if something happens that we did not pray for, we must have no doubt at all that what God wants is more expedient than what we wanted ourselves. Our great Mediator gave us an example of this. After he had said: "Father, if it is possible, let this cup be taken away from me," he immediately added, "Yet not what I will, but what you will."

Our ultimate goal is that our desires become one with God's desires. To the extent that our bargaining, wrestling, and running are manifestations of our denying and doubting, we are still in need of conversion, still in need of growing in trust that God wills only what is best for us. The Spirit prays that our sight will be lengthened and our hearts stretched, and God's grace strengthens us in patient waiting.

In the meantime, we pray:

> God, teach me to want what you want.
> Amen.

When our wills are one with his, we are at peace.

The Present Is Full of God's Presence

Waiting for a flight not long ago, I noticed a middle-aged woman across the concourse, talking and gesturing enthusiastically. She was alone. I glanced opposite her to see if perhaps someone on my side was gesturing back, but I did not see anyone.

When it was time to board the flight, I became aware that the same woman was in line directly in front of me, still talking, still gesturing. It was then I realized she was on a headset cell phone, so small that even up close I could not actually see it. She still appeared to be talking to the air, and even though she was less than a foot in front of me, her gestures pointed to some faraway place.

Once onboard, I couldn't help but overhear every word of the cell-phone conversations of the man seated directly behind me: swimming lessons, the vendor in Kansas City, business strategies, rescheduled meetings. He was on the same flight as I and sixty other passengers, yet his attention was focused elsewhere, many miles distant.

There's no doubt that wireless communication has made things easier for many people, including me. But I wonder if speed and accessibility don't also carry significant hazards. Let me reflect on two of them.

First, instant messages are sent in expectation of instant responses. On the one hand, that such communication is possible is nothing short of miraculous. On the other hand, the expectation of instantaneousness causes everyone's engines to rev up a few thousand revolutions, adding stress to already overloaded lives. I wouldn't be surprised if millions of secretaries (including mine!) would be a little happier if they were not as instantaneously accessible to their bosses and coworkers.

Second, wireless communication has the unfortunate consequence of intentionally diverting our attention from where we actually are at the moment to faraway places, faraway projects. We talk and gesture at the air, and make long-distance arrangements with unseen colleagues, all the while ignoring the people right next to us. Witness the number of people who talk on cell phones while at the wheel.

I'm not a social scientist and leave to others the long-term ramifications of those observations. I am a spiritual leader, however, and I wonder whether the two hazards I mention don't carry with them some perilous spiritual side effects: What do I do if God does not answer my prayers as swiftly as I would like? What if, when I pray, I feel as if I'm speaking to the air and wonder if anyone is listening? What if I attend Mass but don't see myself as taking part in communal prayer? What if my attention is so continuously focused elsewhere that I fail to notice the people, the messages, the blessings, right in front of me?

I have a feeling that much of the time in my prayer, God is trying to begin the conversation by saying, "Peter, slow down. Wait. Look around this chapel. Make yourself present to me. I am already present to you. Presence is more important than words. Waiting for me is the best antidote to the stress of your fast-paced day."

It is quite possible to attend Sunday Mass as if passing through an airport, as if Mass is a private affair conducted in the presence of others, mostly strangers. It is important to remember that "I" participate at Mass as part of a community — the family of God, the Body of Christ, the Church. Many of our parishes are very large. However, no one in my parish is a stranger to me, even if I have never met him or her. As St. Paul wrote, "You are no longer strangers and sojourners, but you are fellow citizens with the holy ones and members of the household of God" (Ephesians 2:19). Greeting one another as we enter church is not only good etiquette — it is also a way of letting God introduce me to my family.

There should be periods of deliberate silence for private prayer during Mass. I personally have always valued those times and think they should be longer. At the same time, Mass is also communal prayer, when "we" pray to our heavenly Father, when "we" are offered to him by Christ, when "we" offer ourselves with Christ. We owe it to God and one another on Sunday morning to give our all to participation at Mass. It is in the Eucharist, more than any other place or time, where God is present to us and gives himself to us in his Son.

We owe it to God and one another on Sunday morning to give our all to participation at Mass.

Wherever I find myself, however — at church, work, shopping, or the airport — there is something which, in this place, at this time, and with these people, God wishes to teach me. If there is a way to apply the word "instantaneous" to the spiritual life, it is that the present, the here-and-now, is bursting with God's presence. It is a hazard to assume that God is somewhere else but not here, or that he should respond to my prayer as quickly as I expect my e-mails to be answered.

It is not because God is far away that we wait for him. We wait for him precisely because he is near, here, in more ways than we can count. We have only to watch, to listen, to notice those around us, and to make ourselves present to him.

Intercession: Sharing in the Prayer of Jesus

As a kid I liked to take things apart: radios, watches, toys, golf balls, furniture. Anything that had an "insides" was fair game. "I wonder what's inside," I would say to myself. "I wonder how that works." There was real science involved, and real reasons why what I took apart was put together in the first place, but I did not discover them at the time.

As the years went by, I did learn a bit of the science behind how things work, and it fascinated and amazed me. But I also learned something even more fascinating and amazing: that there are realities beyond the realm of science, realities so profound that they are felt deep down in one's bones with gut-level certitude but elude any attempts at dissection or scientific analysis. Such are the ways of God.

At times, such realities do not occur to us in certitude but as an interior longing, a question, an intuition, even an ache for something better. We wonder about that which we cannot see but to which we feel an inescapable attraction. "Am I dreaming this up?" we ask ourselves. It is a true grace to recognize eventually that our longing, our question, our intuition, our ache, and our attraction are there because there is Someone to long for, Someone who is the answer, Someone whose very presence we intuited, Someone we ache to know, Someone attracting us to himself.

News came a few years ago that a scientific study had been done on the effectiveness of intercessory prayer, but the results were not awe-inspiring. According to the March 31, 2006, online edition of *Science and Theology News*, "The largest-ever study of prayer offers discouragement to religious believers hoping for evidence that prayer for God's intervention in the natural order is effective. The study ... says that praying for the health of patients from a distance is not effective in reducing complications after heart surgery."

It isn't necessary here to report more about the study. Suffice it to say that such studies miss the point. Prayer cannot be taken apart, analyzed, or scientifically considered. Doing so is tantamount to asking a husband why he loves his wife, or a mother why she loves her children. There is no explanation for love, nor can it be taken apart and scrutinized for its effectiveness. And prayer is about love.

Why do we offer prayers of petition, of intercession? The answer is quite simple: Because Jesus does, without ceasing. Because the Holy Spirit does, without ceasing.

Intercessory prayer is prayer with Jesus and the Holy Spirit. The author of Hebrews writes that Jesus is "always able to save those who approach God through him, since he lives forever to make intercession for them" (Hebrews 7:25). The Holy Spirit "itself intercedes [for us and] ... intercedes for the holy ones according to God's will" (Romans 8:26-27).

The *Catechism of the Catholic Church* explains:

> Since Abraham, intercession — asking on behalf of another — has been characteristic of a heart attuned to God's mercy. In the age of the Church, Christian intercession participates in Christ's, as an expression of the communion of saints. In intercession, he who prays looks "not only to his own interests, but also to the interests of others," even to the point of praying for those who do him harm (Phil 2:4; cf. Acts 7:60; Lk 23:28, 34). (CCC 2635)

Jesus' eternal prayer of intercession is so perfect that even from the cross he prayed for those who harmed him. It is precisely there — on the cross — where the love behind his intercession reveals itself. Jesus longs for all people to come with him to the Father; he seeks only the best for all, and he gave his life for all. His gift of himself on the cross and his eternal prayer of intercession for us are different aspects of the one love he has for us, and his eternal intercession always points to trust in his Father's mercy.

We will never go wrong joining Jesus and the Holy Spirit in interceding for those God loves.

I love the Exodus account (chapter 17) of the Israelites' battle with the Amalekites. As Joshua and his army fought, Moses positioned himself at the top of a hill with Aaron and Hur. As long as Moses kept his hands raised in prayer, Israel had the better of the fight. When he grew tired, they brought a rock for him to sit on, and Aaron and Hur supported his uplifted hands until sunset, one on each side. The Israelites were victorious.

Two beautiful insights emerge from the striking image of the uplifted hands of Moses supported by Aaron and Hur. The first is how we support one another by intercessory prayer, because we are one in trust of God's power and mercy. All of us have our share of trials and need that support.

The second insight is that as great as Moses was, he was still one of us, in need of support as he did God's work. Jesus, on the other hand, raised his hands and allowed them to be stretched out on the cross because he was the Son of God, whose death would save us. We do not support his arms in the victory over death: His upraised, outstretched arms support us, in one eternal and effective act of intercessory prayer.

We will never go wrong joining Jesus and the Holy Spirit in interceding for those God loves — and that means everyone. God's love cannot be analyzed, taken apart, or dissected because it is pure and undivided. God's love never goes without effect.

Giving Ourselves to God More and More

Every now and then, when I spend the night in a hotel or at a friend's house, I awake in the morning and for a brief moment don't know where I am. I'm confused and frustrated until I get my bearings, then I smile at my absentmindedness.

As creatures of habit, we take our bearings in a variety of ways, usually without awareness of how we are doing so. The location of the windows and the door; the sounds of the heating system and the neighbors' dogs; the feel of the carpet or the cold tile on our feet — these sense perceptions become so much a part of our personal landscape that we identify with them in an automatic, spontaneous way. They tell us whether we are at home or lost, safe or in danger, alone or with family and friends.

From a spiritual perspective, intentionally getting our bearings is a good, even necessary, thing to do. We call such an exercise "examen" or "examination of conscience," and we use it as a means of probing and assessing our relationship with God and others. Although we most often associate an examination of conscience with the sacrament of Penance, there is a long tradition in the Church of making it a nightly practice.

We instinctively know that faith is taking us somewhere — that God is taking us somewhere — but perhaps we do not ask often enough whether we are doing all we can to stay on that path, whether we are cooperating with or resisting God's loving tug, whether we have left our friends and families behind in our dusty tracks (because of our insensitivity) or lagged far behind them (because of our laziness).

Examen helps us get our bearings, ensures we are on the path of God, and encourages loving awareness of the people around us. It reminds us that a vibrant relationship with God awakens the deepest resources of our souls and helps us flourish where we are. Examen is about growth — increase in faith and deepening our relationship with God; it is about contrition — sorrow for sin and the experience of God's mercy; it is about love — recognizing the faces and needs of those we already love and opening our hearts to those we have locked out.

An examination of conscience can take a variety of forms. Usually it includes some kind of standard or compass (the Ten Commandments, the Beatitudes, or a specific set of spiritual and moral questions); it ends with the formation of simple resolutions to work on one area or another with the goal of learning how to give God's commands primacy in our lives.

The format could be something like this:

- First, humble ourselves in the presence of God. A favorite Scripture passage can help us attain the proper frame of mind. "Lord, have mercy on me, a sinner." "Lord, if you will, you can make me clean."
- Next, ask for God's light to see ourselves and others as he sees us, light to recognize and acknowledge our weaknesses and the temptations that surround us. Ask for a truly penitent heart, a genuine desire to grow, and the courage to follow through on our resolutions.
- Then, use a particular standard to examine ourselves. We could use either those mentioned above or a simple, personal one, along these lines: Whom have I offended today — God, my family or neighbor, myself? What have I done right, and how can I deepen my desire to do always what is right? What could I have done better? Have I tried to be "successful" on my own, or have I acknowledged to God that I can do nothing without his grace? Do I allow myself to be easily distracted from his ways? Do I thank God and others for the good they have done for me?

- Next, express our sorrow and ask God's pardon. We could make an act of contrition or reflect on another Scripture passage. "A humble and contrite heart, O God, you will not spurn." "Lord, you know everything. You know that I love you."
- Finally, consider ways to grow and improve in the sight of God, and then make a resolution to give attention to certain areas for improvement. Do I need to stay away from specific temptations? Work on a particular virtue — truth, charity, patience, joy? Do I need to give more time to prayer? Notice those around me instead of thinking of myself? Any of these simple questions gives us ample material for tomorrow's discipleship.

At Baptism, we were adopted, through Christ and the Holy Spirit, as children of our heavenly Father. Developing a nightly practice of examen gives the focus we need for a fruitful Christian life by refining our docility to God's commands. It prepares us to receive his grace, mercy, and forgiveness in the sacrament of Reconciliation.

Awareness of our sinfulness and need for God's help is a great blessing because it opens us to his boundless mercy.

We have our bearings and know precisely where we stand when we are mindful of our relationship with God. Awareness of our sinfulness and need for God's help is a great blessing because it opens us to his boundless mercy. The goal of the Christian life, after all, is not to be successful in our good works or penance — it is to give ourselves to God more and more, to be at peace knowing that every morning, no matter where we are, we awake in his loving hands.

Sigh of Sadness — Prayer of Surrender

I once heard someone breathe a sigh from the depths of his soul. In a tragedy that touched the entire parish, a teenager died in an automobile accident as he and two friends were driving back to college. At the funeral Mass, in the stillness after Communion, once the singing had ceased and everyone was seated quietly for prayer, the young man's father breathed a long, deep sigh. Seated in the sanctuary only a few feet from him, I heard and felt it intensely. But the sigh was so profound that it affected everyone in church.

No one could mistake that his was a sigh of sadness, filled with the unspeakable sorrow of parents who have lost a child. So spontaneous and heartfelt was the sigh that it captured what everyone was feeling and infused the congregation with a tangible atmosphere of unity and compassion.

There was also no mistaking, however, that this sigh did something more: It brought healing. It was a kind of catharsis in the presence of God, a spontaneous and heartfelt surrender to God of everything about this heartbreaking tragedy. I'll never forget that moment, with both its sadness and its healing surrender.

I still hear from the young man's parents several times a year. With courage, determination, and the support of church and friends they have moved forward. With loving pride, they still speak of a son lost in his prime, of how he had flowered in college, and of how classmates honored him four years after his death at a graduation ceremony he would never attend. They had every reason to be proud, and they still do. They still miss him, and God understands.

I believe the deep sigh we heard in church that day was the first of many steps forward. Breathed in the presence of God breathed out to God — it was a kind of self-emptying that allowed God's grace to enter and do his delicate work.

Recounting the events surrounding Jesus' death, Matthew and Mark tell us that in his agony Jesus cried out in a loud voice, "*Eli, Eli, lema sabachthani*?" Pouring out everything for our sakes in life and in death, he prayed the opening lines of Psalm 22 (and perhaps the entire psalm): "My God, my God, why have you forsaken me?" (Matthew 27:46; Mark 15:34). He opened his heart, spilling his deepest emotions to his Father in the sight and hearing of all.

The Evangelists describe the moment of Jesus' death in differing but comparable ways. Matthew writes, "Jesus cried out again in a loud voice, and gave up his spirit" (27:50). Mark writes, "Jesus gave a loud cry and breathed his last" (15:37). Luke writes, "Jesus cried out in a loud voice, 'Father, into your hands I commend my spirit'; and when he had said this he breathed his last" (23:46). And John writes, "When Jesus had taken the wine [offered toward his mouth, on a sprig of hyssop], he said, 'It is finished.' And bowing his head, he handed over the spirit" (19:30).

In biblical language, the words "spirit" and "breath" have the same origin. At the point of death, Jesus "breathed his last" and "handed over his spirit." Having prayed in painful agony on the cross ("Why have you abandoned me?"), he sighed, poured out, breathed out, surrendered everything to his Father. Capuchin Father Raniero Cantalamessa, the preacher to the papal household, notes that John intended two meanings when he wrote that Jesus "handed over his spirit": a natural one (he drew his last breath) and a mystical one (he emitted his Holy Spirit). "The last breath of Jesus was the first breath of the Church," says Father Cantalamessa.

The mystical meaning which John intimates was confirmed Easter evening, when Jesus appeared to the apostles in the Upper Room. He "breathed on them and said to them, 'Receive the holy Spirit' " (John 20:22). He had breathed his last in death,

I think Psalm 22 is like a long, deep sigh from the depths of one's soul, a sigh filled with both sadness and healing.

but through the Holy Spirit he breathed new, healed, resurrected life into the Church — and into you and me.

I think Psalm 22 is like a long, deep sigh from the depths of one's soul, a sigh filled with both sadness and healing. Like most psalms, it should be read in its entirety to appreciate what it expresses and where it leads. From the opening line of aching desolation, the psalmist takes us through remembrance of God's faithfulness ("You have been my guide since I was first formed, / my security at my mother's breast"), to prayer for his help ("But you, O Lord, be not far from me; / O my help, hasten to aid me"), to praise for his reply ("I will proclaim your name to my brethren … / For he has not spurned nor disdained the wretched man in his misery … / And to him my soul shall live").

A sigh of sadness that brings healing surrenders everything to God and allows God to show his loving care as he has always done. We need not be facing a tragedy to receive God's healing as we figuratively — or literally — surrender everything to him in a sigh from the depths of our souls. His Spirit, his life-giving breath, will rush in with peace and give us courage to take the next step forward with him.

God Turns His Face Toward Us

There are many reasons why a person might not look another in the eyes: shyness, anger, embarrassment, shame, indifference, preoccupation with a problem, a desire for privacy, etc. In public places, we often do not "face" one another because we have grown accustomed to being in the midst of people we do not know. Though in a crowd, we remain anonymous out of habit. We pass people but do not face them. We see them but do not look them in the eyes.

Our "face" is that side of ourselves which we turn toward others when we enter into a personal relationship with them. Essentially, when we turn our face toward or away from someone, we are indicating whether we want to enter into a relationship — or deny one. A "face-to-face" encounter is so significant that we might tell someone, "I would like to speak to you about this in person rather than over the telephone." To avoid such an encounter is equally significant. Although not looking someone in the eyes may be an expression of our indifference, the gesture itself is never indifferent.

We speak of "facing the facts," "facing reality," "facing the truth," "facing my parents," etc. — and we mean that we intentionally encounter people or situations as they are, that we "see" them directly and fully. Intentionally not to face something or someone means that we are disengaging ourselves from life as it is.

This image is often found in sacred Scripture: "The LORD is just and loves just deeds; / the upright will see his face" (Psalm 11:7); " 'Come,' says my heart, 'seek his face'; / your face, LORD, do I seek!" (Psalm 27:8); "LORD, you showed me favor, / established for me mountains of virtue. / But when you hid your face / I was struck with terror" (Psalm 30:8); "O God, watch over our shield; look upon the face of your anointed" (Psalm 84:10).

When Miriam and Aaron complained to God through jealousy of Moses, God replied:

If there are prophets among you,
    in visions I reveal myself to them,
    in dreams I speak to them;
Not so with my servant Moses!
Throughout my house he is worthy of trust:
    face to face I speak to him,
    plainly and not in riddles.
The likeness of the LORD he beholds. (Numbers 12:6-8)

God never really hides his face from us; however, we often hide our faces from him.

People of biblical times understood the deeply symbolic nature of the image of the "face." Because God's face is turned toward us, we are secure. In fact, "to let one's face shine" on another is a Hebrew idiom for "smile." Not to be face-to-face with God is to feel the deepest kind of insecurity, to be filled with the most unsettling kind of anxiety. The authors of Scripture came to understand that God never really hides his face from us; however, we often hide our faces from him. Thus, they urge us, "Seek his face."

The purest manner of "seeking the face of God" and "being turned toward God" in this life is prayer. God's face is always turned toward us, and with his glance he draws us to himself, inviting us to look him in the eyes.

In heaven, when we are literally face-to-face with God, everything will be clear. In St. Paul's day, mirrors were made not of glass but of polished metal, and their reflection was imperfect. He wrote, "At present we see indistinctly, as in a mirror, but then face to face. At present I know partially; then I shall know fully, as I am fully known" (1 Corinthians 13:12). The beatific vision will be marked by perfect clarity in our encounter with God; and though that encounter might seem dim in this life, it is cleaned and polished through prayer.

Shame, embarrassment, indifference, or anger might tempt us to avoid the face of God, but we are never complete when we are not facing him. God erases our shame, soothes our embarrassment, and melts our indifference. When we engage our relationship with him in prayer, we are complete. Until then, to put it bluntly, things remain hopelessly blurred.

One final point. If we deliberately turn our face from others, we are still in a sense turning our face from God: "If anyone says, 'I love God,' but hates his brother, he is a liar; for whoever does not love a brother whom he has seen cannot love God whom he has not seen" (1 John 4:20).

As we see how God has looked us in the eyes and revealed his infinite love through Jesus, we turn our face to him in prayer. As we meet him face-to-face and deepen our friendship with him, he teaches us to love as he loves — to notice others as we pass them on the street, to have compassion for the poor Lazarus at the gate, to forgive those who have harmed us, to turn our selfishness into self-giving:

> The LORD bless you and keep you!
> The LORD let his face shine upon you, and be gracious
> to you!
> The LORD look upon you kindly and give you peace!
> (Numbers 6:22-26)

God has smiled on us. As we seek his face, may we find it in prayer and love.

Called to Intimate Love

Someone once remarked that I seem to know the words of many hymns by heart. To an extent that's true, but after the second verse I usually end up humming along if a hymnal isn't nearby.

Thirty-plus years of seminary and ministry have accustomed my brain to the words of many popular hymns. However, I have discovered that the "old" versions, with "thee" and "thou," are the first to come from my lips. When the verses have been modernized to read "you," I have to do some fast thinking. To be honest, I wonder if we haven't lost something by fiddling with old hymns in that way.

Until recently, I had always regarded "thee" and "thou" as formal expressions of respect for God, the way we once expressed the vast difference between God and us. But their meaning is exactly the opposite of what I had thought. In Middle English (in use from the twelfth through the fifteenth century), "you" was the formal way to address another person. "Thou" was the informal way to address loved ones, parents, close friends, and children. It was the word used with those closest to us, with whom we had an intimate relationship — and it is precisely for that reason that it was used when speaking or singing to God.

English translations of psalms and hymns referred to God as "thou" not because he is distant and unreachable, but because he is a close friend, an intimate! As Jesus taught his disciples, that is the kind of relationship his heavenly Father extends to us all.

When I visited the Holy Land many years ago, my tour included a day at the Dead Sea, the lowest place on earth. The Jordan River empties into the Dead Sea, and because there are no tributaries leading out of the sea, the heat evaporates much of the water, leaving heavy salt and mineral deposits. One has to wear sandals to wade in the shallow water, because the seabed is lined with sharp stones.

The day we visited, I noticed that a small child had strayed from his family and was tiptoeing painfully on the rocks. He began to cry out to his dad for help. "*Abba*!" he screamed tearfully. It dawned on me for the first time what it means that Jesus taught us to call his Father "Abba."

In his agony, Jesus prayed, "Abba, Father, all things are possible to you. Take this cup away from me, but not what I will but what you will" (Mark 14:36). "*Abba*" is Aramaic (the language spoken by Jesus), and when St. Mark wrote his gospel in Greek, he preferred to keep the Aramaic expression, because it revealed the intimacy of Son and Father. Children used "*Abba*" to speak to their dads, and the early Church took up the same use.

St. Paul wrote, "As proof that you are children, God sent the spirit of his Son into our hearts, crying out, 'Abba, Father!' So you are no longer a slave but a child, and if a child then also an heir, through God" (Galatians 4:6-7).

Jesus used another expression to teach his disciples about their relationship to him:

> "No one has greater love than this, to lay down one's life for one's friends. You are my friends if you do what I command you. I no longer call you slaves, because a slave does not know what his master is doing. I have called you friends, because I have told you everything I have heard from my Father." (John 15:13-15)

Because we are adopted children of the Father, friends and brothers and sisters of Jesus, we can cry out with the divine Son of God, "Abba!"

God, through whom everything exists and without whom nothing exists, who created the universe and all that is in it, who breathed life into us and saved us from sin, who is the perfection of knowledge and freedom and truth, does not want to be distant from us. Instead, he invites every one of us to intimate love and friendship. So great is his love that he gave us his Son. The Son revealed to us the extraordinary familiarity and intimate love of the Father. The Holy Spirit sustains us in unity with Father and Son.

The Son revealed to us the extraordinary familiarity and intimate love of the Father.

There is no disrespect in addressing God the way we do our closest friends and loved ones. In fact, that is how he introduces himself. Blessed are we when we accept his hand in friendship and nourish that friendship with prayer and love. Nothing in this life is more powerful.

Now, if "thee" and "thou" fall spontaneously from my lips when singing a memorized hymn, I'm glad I trip on the words, because I'm reminded of an insight from a trip to the Dead Sea and a simple English lesson. After all, the point is not the words, but the love.

Thanks be to thee, my Lord Jesus Christ,
For all the benefits thou hast won for me,
For all the pains and insults thou hast borne for me.
O merciful Redeemer, Friend, and Brother,
May I know thee more clearly,
Love thee more dearly,
And follow thee more nearly:
For ever and ever. Amen.
(St. Richard of Chichester)

Responding to the God Who Has Chosen Me

I have often been struck by a theme that emerges frequently in the readings of the liturgy: We are chosen by God.

> You are a people holy to the LORD, your God; the LORD, your God, has chosen you from all the peoples on the face of the earth to be a people specially his own. (Deuteronomy 7:6)

> "We are your people and your inheritance, O Lord.... Hear us whenever we call upon you, because you have set us apart among all the peoples of the earth for your inheritance." (1 Kings 8:51-53)

> You have seen for yourselves how I bore you up on eagle wings and brought you here to myself. (Exodus 19:4)

The Church invites us to remember that God has chosen us and made us his people, his beloved, and he has taken care of us in ways far beyond our understanding. He has been faithful to us even when we rejected him; he has not turned his back on us even when we have turned our backs on him. He promised to supply all our needs, and he has never gone back on that promise. In other words, we are reminded that when God chooses us, he stands by us through thick and thin. As that truth shines on us and rolls around a bit in our hearts, questions naturally arise:

Has God chosen me — does God love me? Even the psalmist grappled with this fundamental question: "What is man

God's love for us is strong, true, faithful, and personal.

that you are mindful of him?" (Psalm 8:5). Although we might wonder at times if God knows us individually — if he knows and cares for me — Scripture makes clear that his love for us is strong, true, faithful, and personal. Read Psalm 139: "LORD, you have probed me, you know me: / you know when I sit and stand; / you understand my thoughts from afar. / You sift through my travels and my rest; / with all my ways you are familiar" (vv. 1-3).

Have I placed emphasis on myself, telling myself that it was I who first chose God? We have a tendency to think everything begins with us and depends on us. However, if I assume that it was I who chose God and not vice versa, I will never understand the meaning of grace — God's initiative-taking love, friendship, and assistance — freely, unexpectedly, and undeservedly offered. Jesus reminded his disciples that it was not they who chose him, but he who chose them. God does ask our response (which in a sense we might call our "choice"), but it is he who first chooses, he who acts first.

As I ask God to hear my prayers, do I take time to listen to his response? No doubt God is accustomed to our talkativeness. Jesus urged persistence in prayer, and St. Paul bid us pray without ceasing. However, prayer is a dialogue, and as we pour out our hearts to him, God asks us to be calm and listen. Perhaps we worry that if we don't keep reminding God of our request, he will forget it — or if we are not fretting about our concerns in prayer (emphasis on the fretting!), we are somehow not doing our part. Usually when we talk incessantly in prayer, we do so because we are holding on tightly to our troubles while telling God about them.

St. Peter offers an alternative route: "Cast all your worries upon him because he cares for you" (1 Peter 5:7). Once we have told God of our needs and concerns in prayer — once we have cast our worries on him — we should be still, confident that he has heard us, and full of hope. The time we spent in fretting can now be spent in peaceful stillness, listening to him.

Have I stood by God through thick and thin, or have I too easily given up on him? This question challenges us to be patient as God works. God does not toy with us, nor does he offer quick fixes; he works deeply, lastingly, within. The Letter of James assures us: "Be patient ... until the coming of the Lord. See how the farmer waits for the precious fruit of the earth, being patient with it until it receives the early and the late rains" (James 5:7).

Have I trusted in God's promise to supply my needs, or have I placed my trust elsewhere — just in case God does not come through for me? Do I hesitate to give my life entirely to God because I do not have the confidence that God is capable of making me completely happy? That is an incisive question worth pondering. Much of our self-reliance, our seeking of false gods, our worry, our over-talkativeness in prayer, and our impatience with God might have its root in our lack of confidence that God is capable of making us completely happy.

Not only is God capable of making us completely happy — only he can make us completely happy. That is why we need to be reminded that he has chosen us and loves us, that he will stand by us and never abandon us, and that he will supply all our needs. If we have gone far afield looking for happiness, today is the time to return to the One who loves each of us as the apple of his eye.

Chapter 5

Sharing in the Fruit of the Cross

Deeply Rooted — Supported by Love

I wonder: How deep into the ground was Jesus' cross planted? It would have had to be deep enough to support the cross and Jesus' added weight.

I wonder: Who dug the hole? Someone yanked from the crowd, a Roman soldier, or a professional who did such things for a living? Was he told to keep digging after the supervisor checked his work and found it unsatisfactory? Did he know who would be raised on the cross to be lodged in the hole he was digging? Did he care?

Or was the hole a permanent one, fixed hard by rocks and mortar, a sign that crucifixions were commonplace in those days?

Whoever dug that hole, he must have dug deep. It had to be a snug fit. It had to be reliable.

Perhaps such questions seem odd. I've been pondering them lately for two reasons: first, because of some words of Jesus; and second, because of some words of Monsignor James E. O'Connell.

Jesus had said to Nicodemus, "Just as Moses lifted up the serpent in the desert, so must the Son of Man be lifted up, so that everyone who believes in him may have eternal life" (John 3:14–15;

see also John 8:28). He was referring to God's instructions to Moses (Numbers 21:9) to fashion a bronze serpent and hold it high on a pole, so that the Israelites who looked up at it would be healed of the serpent bites God had sent as a reproach.

In John 12:32-33, Jesus said to a crowd: "And when I am lifted up from the earth, I will draw everyone to myself." John adds, "He said this indicating the kind of death he would die."

Monsignor James E. O'Connell, the revered senior priest of the Diocese of Little Rock who died at age ninety-seven in 2005, was known as an extraordinary orator. One of his former high school students (now in his eighties) told me that Monsignor O'Connell frequently said to them, "Boys, if you want to go high, dig deep."

I like the phrase because it has many applications. If we want to do well in life, we must have deep roots. Otherwise what we build will soon collapse because its foundation is weak.

In the past few weeks, Monsignor O'Connell's words have shed light for me on the Scripture passages I just quoted. If Jesus was "lifted up" on the cross, the cross must have been planted deep into the arid ground to remain standing for so many hours. It is a gruesome thought, but no doubt someone was charged with ensuring that such was the case every time there was a crucifixion. Otherwise crosses would have tumbled to the ground, their victims with them, only to require replanting with backbreaking, frustrating effort.

The cross dug deep into the earth because it stood so high. But even more was Jesus deeply, steadfastly rooted in his heavenly Father. How else could he have stood firm through the ridicule, the scourges, the false testimony, his passion and death? How could the cross have stood tall, bearing Jesus' bodily weight and the much more burdensome weight of our sins, had Jesus not been deeply grounded in his Father?

Jesus sought every opportunity to be one with his Father in prayer, to be strengthened in his mission, to give himself for

The cross was planted deep in the earth, for Jesus was planted deep in loving trust of his Father.

our sakes and his Father's glory. There was nothing superficial about Jesus, nothing artificial, nothing opportunistic, no trace of self-preservation. Only love could have sustained him through his ordeal, love for his Father and love for us. Uncompromising love. Unshakable love. Deep love.

When Paul wrote that we must have the attitude of Christ, he quoted a hymn familiar to his fellow Christians:

> Have among yourselves the same attitude that is also yours in Christ Jesus,
>
> Who, though he was in the form of God,
> did not regard equality with God something to be grasped.
> Rather, he emptied himself,
> taking the form of a slave,
> coming in human likeness;
> and found human in appearance,
> he humbled himself,
> becoming obedient to death,
> even death on a cross.
> Because of this, God greatly exalted him
> and bestowed on him the name
> that is above every name,
> that at the name of Jesus
> every knee should bend,
> of those in heaven and on earth and under the earth.
> (Philippians 2:5-10)

Paul echoes what John teaches about Jesus' death: that through the cross Jesus was exalted, glorified, and raised — "lifted up" —

by his heavenly Father. The Church always speaks of his "death and resurrection" in the same breath, because Jesus' submission to death out of love for us is at the same time the glorious triumph of his Father's love for all. Sin cannot stand up to such love. Death cannot conquer the creator of life.

The cross was planted deep in the earth, for Jesus was planted deep in loving trust of his Father, deep in his determination to free us from sin and death. As we bear the crosses life gives us, we can recall the depth that gave Jesus strength, the depth through which his Father "greatly exalted" him. When we sink our roots deep in God, he upholds us, strengthens us, and gives us life, though we had begun to think all was lost.

When on the last day our bodies rise up glorious in Christ, we will see just how deep his cross was planted in the earth — for his sacrifice at Calvary was complete enough for all and forever.

Pain Is Healed in Works of Self-Giving

Rabbi Harold S. Kushner recounts a venerable Chinese tale about an elderly woman whose only son died. Inconsolable, she went to a holy man to ask how to bring him back to life. Instead of offering false hope, however, the holy man instructed her to bring him a mustard seed from a home that had never known sorrow. A seed from such a home would surely help banish sadness from her life.

Beginning her search, she knocked on the door of a mansion, reasoning that such a home would be just what she was looking for. But the owners quickly told her otherwise. "You have definitely come to the wrong place," they said, for their lives had been filled with sadness similar to hers. She listened with compassion to their story.

"Who better than I," she said to herself, "would be able to help this family, for I understand what they are going through?" Before moving on, she comforted them with love from the depths of her heart, for indeed their story was hers.

Soon she discovered that every home, palace, and shack knew its share of sadness. At each stop, she offered consolation, and soon her sorrow vanished. Her pain had been healed by works of love.

I have always enjoyed reading the lives of the saints, and as I grow older, my affection for them grows. Aristocrats and paupers, women and men, priests, religious, and lay, their lives often offer the witness of pain and sorrow transformed by faith and love. Our communion with the saints is a vehicle of hope, because in them we find life experiences common to many.

Rita Lotti was born at Roccaporena, near Cascia, Italy, in 1381, the only child of Antonio and Amata. Her parents were

Through love and constancy and faith, God can heal all wounds.

revered as official reconcilers in their small town and earned the title "Peacemakers of Jesus Christ." Rita eventually married Paulo Mancini, a town watchman who was often caught in physical conflicts between rival factions. According to some accounts, Paolo was harsh and ill-tempered, and married life was difficult for Rita. Two sons were born to their marriage, and after Paolo was murdered, they vowed to avenge their father's death.

Despite Rita's pleading, her sons would not let go of their desire for revenge, and she placed her anxiety about them in God's hands. When they died, both had been reconciled with God. After some years as a widow known for her works of charity, Rita applied for admission to an Augustinian convent but was refused three times, in part out of fear that the violence surrounding her family would affect convent life.

Taking up the peacemaking role of her parents once again, Rita worked skillfully to reconcile Paolo's family with the family of those responsible for his death, and the two families eventually signed a document formalizing their reconciliation. Rita entered religious life and died in 1457. She was canonized in 1900, and her feast day is May 22, and many often ask her intercession when praying for reconciliation within their families.

A prayer on the feasts of saints includes these words:

[Y]ou are praised in the company of your Saints....
By their way of life you offer us an example,
by communion with them you give us companionship,
by their intercession, sure support,
so that, encouraged by so great a cloud of witnesses,
we may run as victors in the race before us....
(Preface I of Saints)

There is no home that has never known sorrow, but Christian history is filled with stories of those who allowed God to turn their sorrow into joy, even in the hardest, hopeless cases. Holy ones like Rita of Cascia, and the holy ones we have known in our own lives, teach us to place our hope in God. Through love and constancy and faith, God can heal all wounds. But more than that, when we truly turn our sorrows over to him, he can make us holy, too.

Handing Ourselves Over to God

Wedged inconspicuously into the corner of his workstation so that only he can see it, a small portrait of Matt Talbot reminds a good friend to take one day at a time and offer God the consistency he desires. The image was given him years ago by his sponsor in Alcoholics Anonymous, a fellow Catholic who had found in Talbot a good role model and inspiration to maintain sobriety.

Matt Talbot was born in Dublin in 1856, into a life of poverty. By the age of 13, he was addicted to alcohol — hopelessly so, according to those who knew him. Desperate at age 28, he made a pledge of sobriety on his knees. With the help of a priest friend, with whom he began to meet weekly, he established and maintained a disciplined program of recovery and remained sober for forty years. Many have remarked that the regimen closely foreshadowed the twelve-step program of Alcoholics Anonymous developed years after his death.

Talbot's healing took place through prayer, fasting, and joy-filled service to others. He never escaped poverty, partly because he gave so much money away. His sister once said, "Matt had no time for money." He preferred to remain in the background, silently but faithfully at Mass and private prayer, quietly tending to those in need. "It is consistency God wants," he is often quoted as saying.

He worked in the timber yards of Dublin and developed a keen sense of his fellow workers' struggle for justice. A union leader described him as "a beacon of light to Irish workers." Matt Talbot died on June 7, 1925, on the way to Mass. He was declared venerable in 1975, and Pope John Paul II (who as a young man once wrote a paper about him) described Talbot as a model of hope for those with substance addictions.

My friend faced his own alcoholism as a young husband and father, increasingly aware that the disease was affecting his health and that of his family. He connected with A.A., began to work his program every day, and has been sober for many years. Much of his free time is spent helping others remain sober as well.

One evening after a parish meeting, one of my sisters was having small talk with her parish priest and a fellow parishioner. The subject arose of asking St. Anthony's intercession when having lost something. My sister added, "In our family, when we lost something, we always asked Matt Talbot to help us find it."

I can confirm her recollection. As clear as a bell, I can hear Mom say, "Ask Matt Talbot to help you." Talbot had become a patron of our dad almost sixty years ago, after he had joined A.A., and Mom was always grateful for his intercession for all the needs of our family. The night of the parish meeting, my sister learned something new about Talbot's dealings through and beyond our family.

After she told her friends about asking Talbot's intercession, her fellow parishioner added, "I know. It was your dad who introduced us to Matt Talbot." Her deceased husband was also in A.A., and soon after he started working the program, some nuns had given him a small portrait of Talbot. "Your dad had given it to the nuns," she said, adding, "When my husband started sponsoring John Smith in A.A., he gave the picture to him, and he still has it."

My sister sent me an e-mail that night telling me about her encounter, because she knows that John Smith and I are good friends; I forwarded the e-mail to him. He was amazed to learn that the picture of Matt Talbot wedged into an inconspicuous corner of his office originally belonged to my dad.

But in another sense, he was not amazed at all.

As a Catholic who prays daily and actively lives his faith, as a recovering alcoholic who daily places his sobriety in God's hands,

Matt Talbot could have given up, but instead he gave himself to God.

and as one who has experienced firsthand the communion that is ours with Christian witnesses living and dead, he saw what I told him as another reason to keep moving forward, keep trusting in God's grace, keep encouraging others, and keep being aware of the "cloud of witnesses" to which the Letter to the Hebrews refers — our sisters and brothers who urge us and encourage us to follow the Lord.

What strikes me about Matt Talbot and the reason the Church is considering his cause for sainthood is this: He is a model of Christian life and holiness not because things came easy for him, but precisely because in poverty, addiction, desperation, and utter helplessness he gave himself entirely to God; not because he achieved something great, but because he allowed God to achieve something great in him. He could have given up, but instead he gave himself to God. God wants what is best for us and asks that we cooperate with his grace, with what he is lovingly doing for us and in us. The struggle to do so — to let go and let God — can be mighty indeed.

Of the many prayer requests I receive, a significant percentage are for those who suffer addictions of various kinds. Perhaps they fear that somehow they are unworthy of God's attention, that they have squandered their chance to receive his grace and healing. Matt Talbot's example and prayers say otherwise and remind us that every human struggle can be the path to holiness and heroic Christian witness if we hand ourselves over to God:

> Therefore, since we are surrounded by so great a cloud of witnesses, let us rid ourselves of every burden and sin that clings to us and persevere in running the race that lies before us while keeping our eyes fixed on Jesus, the leader and perfecter of faith. For the sake of the joy that

lay before him he endured the cross, despising its shame, and has taken his seat at the right of the throne of God. Consider how he endured such opposition from sinners, in order that you may not grow weary and lose heart. (Hebrews 12:1-3)

Bringing Comfort and Peace to Those in Fear

Three hundred sixty-seven feet long and five thousand six hundred eighty tons heavy, the *Dorchester* was launched as a luxury passenger ship in 1926 by the Merchant and Miners Transportation Company of Baltimore. Advertised as the equal of the finest hotels, it could provide three hundred passengers with the best of creature comforts and entertainment, including a casino, as it cruised the American East Coast from Florida to New York.

By March 1942, German U-boats were destroying Allied ships in the North Atlantic, and our government was caught unprepared. The *Dorchester* — along with countless other vessels of myriad designs, purposes, conditions, and ages — was called into service. As a crowded troop carrier, the USAT *Dorchester* ferried servicemen, merchant seamen, and civilian workers to their duties in the arctic — and strategic — wilderness of Greenland.

Their precious human cargo a favorite target of the stealthy U-boats, troop carriers were typically protected by a convoy. The evening of February 2, 1943, the Greenland-bound USAT *Dorchester*, with nine hundred two aboard, left Newfoundland with two other ships, escorted by three Coast Guard cutters. At 12:55 a.m. the following morning, some one hundred miles from its destination, the USAT *Dorchester* was struck amidships by a torpedo fired deftly from U-223. Twenty-seven minutes later, the *Dorchester* slid beneath the Atlantic, taking many of its passengers with it.

Eventually, two hundred thirty-one survivors were plucked from the icy waters, their survival seen as miracle after miracle. Of those miracles recounted through the years, many are known to be the result of the selfless heroism of four clergymen now often referred to as "The Four Chaplains."

By God's providence, the four were assigned to the USAT *Dorchester* on its last cruise: Lt. George L. Fox, a Methodist minister; Lt. Alexander D. Goode, a rabbi; Lt. Clark V. Poling, a Dutch Reformed minister; and Lt. John P. Washington, a Catholic priest. The four had already formed a bond during a hurried chaplains' school at Harvard and were pleased to be together on the *Dorchester*. With uncommon charism and talent, they formed a dynamic team that gave comfort and courage to frightened young men more than aware of the dangers lurking in the Atlantic in early 1943.

When the torpedo hit early on February 3, they sprang into action, guiding the men through the darkness to deck and lifeboats, encouraging them calmly and at times firmly to follow orders and abandon ship. Topside, they distributed lifejackets to men who had none, and when the lifejackets ran out, the chaplains removed their own and gave them away. "It was the finest thing I have seen or hope to see this side of heaven," said survivor John Ladd. Testimony from others recounts that as the ship sank, the chaplains were arm-in-arm, braced against the slanting deck; through the darkness they could be heard praying, each in his own tradition.

My sister, Sister Marian, a Dominican of the Congregation of St. Cecilia in Nashville, tells me that Father John Washington was the nephew of Sister Ann Washington of their community. The older sisters remember him bounding up the front steps when he visited and playing the piano to entertain them. Sister Margaret Mary recalls that her blood sister, Sister Joseph Marie, was sent with Sister Ann to be with Father Washington's mother when word came that he was lost at sea.

All four chaplains were posthumously awarded the Distinguished Service Cross and Purple Heart in 1944. The Special

"Have we not all one Father? Hath not one God created us?" (Malachi 2:10)

Medal for Heroism was authorized by Congress and posthumously awarded by the president in 1961 — the only time the award has ever been given. In 1998, a resolution sailed unanimously through the House and Senate to designate February 3 as Four Chaplains Day. The Four Chaplains are memorialized across the country in numerous ways, including stained-glass windows at the Pentagon, the Washington National Cathedral, and St. Stephen Church in Kearny, New Jersey, where Father Washington served as assistant pastor. The lobby of a public school named for Rabbi Goode in York, Pennsylvania, features a mural with the likenesses of the chaplains and an inscription from the prophet Malachi in Hebrew, Latin, and English:

> Have we not all one Father?
> Hath not one God created us?
> Why do we deal treacherously every man against his brother,
> by profaning the covenant of our fathers? (2:10)

I recommend reading *No Greater Glory: The Four Immortal Chaplains and the Sinking of the Dorchester in World War II*, by Dan Kurzman. Faith and Values Media has also produced an inspiring documentary about the chaplains.

When we mark Four Chaplains Day each February 3, let's pray that people of faith around the world will unite as the chaplains did, to bring peace and comfort to all in danger and fear.

In Stress and Frustration, God's Grace Is Sufficient

"It's not about the ice, is it?" his wife said to him. Watching a high school football game one fall night a few years ago, I chatted with a team doctor in between injuries. We solved the world's problems and at one point discussed how we deal — or don't deal — with stress. He told a story on himself.

Tied in emotional knots after a particularly frustrating day, he arrived home for supper. He probably closed the door a little too vigorously, probably sighed a little too conspicuously, probably greeted the kids a little too brusquely. They noticed but said nothing. He went to the kitchen, ostensibly to help his wife set the table, the day's stress noticeably dragging behind him. His presence chilled the room.

When he placed the first glass under the ice dispenser, nothing happened. Growling, he tried again, more forcefully. "What's wrong with this icemaker?" he snapped to no one in particular but in earshot of everyone. "Why don't you get this thing fixed?" he indirectly directed his wife.

Turning from the stove, she walked over to the refrigerator, where his hand was still lodged with a glass in the dispenser. Gently taking the glass from his hand and looking him straight in the eye, she said calmly, "It's not about the ice, is it?"

She nailed him. No, it wasn't about the ice at all. It was about a bad day, a non-compliant patient, a feeling of failure, a sense of disappointment in himself — a lot of pent-up stuff that erupted in front of the Frigidaire. Once he told her what the day was like, he understood what was going on inside himself, and no, it wasn't about the ice at all. His true frustrations on the table and soothed by an open ear, he could laugh at himself. And everyone could enjoy dinner.

I appreciated his story because we both understood how things can so easily get twisted within and around us, and how a nagging worry or family concern can leave us pointing fingers and grousing at everyone in the vicinity. And we don't even know why.

A nagging worry or family concern can leave us pointing fingers and grousing at everyone in the vicinity. And we don't even know why.

At times, we are puzzles to ourselves. We ask why we said this or did that. Likewise, when a coworker or family member thunders past us, leaving an angry cloud of dust in his or her wake, we wonder what's going on inside. I used to joke with a priest who served as principal of a high school that I could always tell when he had had a bad day, because about six p.m. he would slam the door to the garage and start cleaning the rectory.

Apparently St. Paul surprised himself repeatedly. To the Corinthians he wrote about the thorn in the flesh that afflicted and exasperated him (2 Corinthians 12), and to the Romans he wrote, "What I do, I do not understand. For I do not do what I want, but I do what I hate" (Romans 7:15). Like the rest of us, he would have preferred to find the "off " switch to struggles within and without, but such a switch did not and does not exist.

For at least some of the unnamed stressors of the day, there is a simple antidote: reflection. And for all of them, there is God's response, the same he gave to Paul: "My grace is sufficient for you, for power is made perfect in weakness" (2 Corinthians 12:9).

I learned a few years ago that when in the course of the day I find myself worried or irritable, aware of a shadow following me around, a moment of private reflection helps put things in perspective. I ask myself one question: "What happened today to create that cloud, to make me feel this way?" Almost always I can identify something — an angry letter, worry about a loved one, a word spoken but later regretted — that I had been dragging through the day. Identifying it and asking God to shed his light on it, I get out from under the cloud and move freely through the day.

But there is also a kind of permanent life stance that Paul eventually learned to take, that of trusting in God's strength and not one's own.

> I will rather boast most gladly of my weaknesses, in order that the power of Christ may dwell with me. Therefore, I am content with weaknesses, insults, hardships, persecutions, and constraints, for the sake of Christ; for when I am weak, then I am strong. (2 Corinthians 12:9-10)

There is a venerated Catholic tradition worth reviving, the "Morning Offering." I learned it as a child, and I have lived in many rectories where the prayer was pasted on the bathroom mirror:

> O Jesus, through the Immaculate Heart of Mary, I offer you all my prayers, works, joys, and sufferings of this day, for all the intentions of your Sacred Heart, in union with the Holy Sacrifice of the Mass throughout the world, in reparation for my sins, for the intentions of all my relatives and friends, and in particular for the intentions of the Holy Father.

A prayer of self-offering takes the focus — and the burden — off ourselves.

A day can so easily become all about "me." By offering it to "Him," we gain direction and focus. Gradually, we learn to recognize God's presence even in the midst of stress, and we hear him whisper repeatedly, "My grace is sufficient for you."

Leaning on Jesus in Time of Temptation

There is not one of us who is not confronted with temptation — temptation to pride, to selfishness, to unjust anger, to lust, to greed, to laziness, to an unforgiving heart. The list of temptations can be long and varies from one person to the next.

We are often confused by temptation. We might say to ourselves, "Was that a sin, or was it a temptation?" "Did I think about that too long, did I cross that line from temptation to sin?" Perhaps we think that in order to be good, we have to rid ourselves of all temptation, of any thought that has even the hint of evil. We think we will have it together when "those thoughts" stop popping into our minds. But soon we find that it is impossible to exercise perfect control over thoughts and emotions.

Temptation is tricky for many reasons — and not only because it can lead us to evil. It is tricky because through it the devil can knock us off center, make us lose confidence in God, discourage us, and persuade us to give up. Scripture makes it clear that the devil's ultimate goal is to cause us to turn away from God, to have us so totally confused that we do not know which end is up. He would like us to literally "get lost," or at least to feel lost.

We must take sin seriously, and we must take temptation seriously, but we must also understand the difference between the two.

The Book of Genesis teaches about our origin in God, our goodness, and the story of our fall from grace. One of the most basic truths that Genesis reveals is that because of a fundamental misuse of freedom, our first parents caused a rupture between our original purpose and our actions so that often we are drawn to what is not good for us.

We must take sin seriously, and we must take temptation seriously, but we must also understand the difference between the two.

Sometimes we are surprised at ourselves, at what our minds can dream up, at our reactions to certain situations, even at attitudes and thoughts diametrically opposed to what we believe and hold dear. This basic brokenness within us is the result of original sin. Jesus was tempted by Satan to go against what his Father had sent him to do, but he did not sin. He chose not the way that made himself the center of the universe, but the way that revealed his Father as the origin, purpose, and sustainer of all things. He chose to give his Father glory.

Often, when we are confronted with temptation, we try to summon willpower to withstand it. At times, we try so hard that the temptation seems to get worse and weighs even more heavily on our minds. Confronted with temptation, we have two choices, like Jesus: to give in and make ourselves the center of the world, or to take a step of faith in the direction of God.

Temptation is not the same as sin. Although it is one of the most basic experiences of being human, we take it seriously because it is the presentation of an important choice. As Father Benedict Groeschel once wrote, each time I resist temptation I am choosing to give glory to God. It is much better to place the struggle with temptation in this positive light: Temptation presents a clear opportunity to give God glory. That does not always make it easier, but it does make what is at stake more obvious.

If the Lord himself was beset by temptations — and the Letter to the Hebrews reminds us that he was tempted in every way that we are, though never sinned — then we should not be surprised when we experience the same. Nor should we be surprised that temptations remain and often increase at a time we have been exceptionally good, prayed more often, read more Scripture, attended Mass more frequently, and so on.

That is the devil's ploy! He wants to discourage us from drawing close to God. He wants us to forget our origin and purpose, to think only of ourselves. It is not that he wants us to be happy with him — he wants us to be unhappy, because he knows how much God loves us.

The measure of our goodness is not the infrequency of temptation — good disciples are not good because they are never tempted. Good disciples are those who lean on Jesus in time of temptation.

Moreover, as St. Augustine once wrote, Jesus made us one with himself when he chose to be tempted by Satan, and in him we share victory over temptation:

> If in Christ we have been tempted, in him we overcome the devil. Do you think only of Christ's temptations and fail to think of his victory? See yourself as tempted in him, and see yourself as victorious in him. He could have kept the devil from himself; but if he were not tempted he could not teach you how to triumph over temptation.

Ironically, the way we deal with temptation gives us a great opportunity for fulfillment, because the more we choose God's way, the more we will learn that sin will never make us happy. Only going in the direction of God, who loves us, makes us happy. The devil does not care about us in the least.

There is no better way to fight temptation and overcome sin than to keep trying. Nothing insults Satan more than our undying faith and hope in the mercy of God.

Never Stop Seeking God

Mother Teresa: Come Be My Light is a collection of personal letters written over a span of many years, which reveal Mother Teresa's experience of darkness and the seeming absence of God. The book is edited with commentary by a member of the order she founded (the Missionaries of Charity), who serves as the "postulator" (official promoter) of her cause for canonization. A newer book, *I Loved Jesus in the Night*, is a personal reflection on the same subject by Dominican Father Paul Murray, who also knew Mother Teresa well.

Both books unveil Mother Teresa's experience of what St. John of the Cross referred to as the "dark night" of the soul, an experience of aloneness and desolation which many have undergone as they have sought to grow spiritually. The "dark night" is a stage in spiritual growth, and its duration varies greatly from person to person. Some have known a dark night of many years, and that was apparently the experience of Mother Teresa.

As a seminarian in Rome in the mid-1970s, I volunteered at a homeless shelter sponsored by the Missionaries of Charity. One week I learned that "Mother" was in the building, and the sisters encouraged me and a friend to meet her. We were escorted to the chapel, where we waited.

We could hear her speaking on the telephone in the next room, and when she had finished she quietly entered the rear of the chapel. As we turned to greet her, she said, "I am sorry I made you wait." I do not recall what we spoke about or how long we spoke, but her humble introduction has stuck with me: "I am sorry I made you wait." Each person, including young men like us whom she did not know, was important to her.

Ten years later, as a priest in Memphis, I had occasion to meet her when she came to town to discuss the possibility of opening a mission in the inner city. I had the privilege of driving her around town with our bishop. He and I sat up front, she and her assistant in back. "We will open a house here, and one in Moscow, and one in Beijing," she said. Her companion interrupted, "But Mother, where will we get all the sisters to run these houses?" "God will provide them," Mother replied.

I now realize that I witnessed these simple but extraordinary expressions of faith during the years she was experiencing the desolation of the spiritual desert. Reflecting on that contrast, I realize that her dedication to God endured and persisted mightily despite her painful inner dryness. That she continued to give herself to Jesus throughout those many years is a testimony of her love for him. She accepted the grace of her vocation and followed him, loved him, served him, and sought him in the poorest of the poor. She would not turn away from Jesus or abandon his beloved poor.

Pope Gregory the Great (late sixth and early seventh century) reflected in one of his homilies on the witness of Mary Magdalene. When Mary went to the tomb and did not find the Lord's body, she thought it had been removed and told the disciples so. After they had seen for themselves that the tomb was empty, the disciples went home, but Mary remained standing outside the tomb. Gregory wrote:

> We should reflect on Mary's attitude and the great love she felt for Christ; for though the disciples had left the tomb, she remained. She was still seeking the one she had not found; and while she sought, she wept; burning with the fire of love, she longed for him who she thought had been taken away.
>
> And so it happened that the woman who stayed behind to seek Christ was the only one to see him. For perseverance is essential to any good deed.

He continued, "At first she sought but did not find, but when she persevered it happened that she found what she was looking for. When our desires are not satisfied, they grow stronger, and becoming stronger they take hold of their object."

Mary Magdalene did not abandon the empty tomb, lonely and desolate as she was, to think that her Lord had died and his body had been stolen. She remained to wait for him, desire him, seek him — even in the darkness of a tomb. It seems that Mother Teresa persisted in seeking her Lord in the excruciating darkness he invited her to enter.

"Burning with the fire of love, she longed for him who she thought had been taken away."
(Pope Gregory the Great)

Most of us experience periods of dryness, darkness, and doubt in our relationship with God, and they should not shock us (or worse, cause us to turn away from God). The example of Mary Magdalene, St. John of the Cross, and Mother Teresa reminds us to never stop seeking God. He is always there, and somehow according to his plan, in the way that is best for each of us, he uses our dark nights to draw us closer.

Every chapel of the Missionaries of Charity across the world has a small sign posted next to the crucifix, which bears the words of Christ on the cross: "I thirst."

Christ on the cross suffered a cruel thirst. The poor endure thirst and hunger beyond our imagining. Mother Teresa thirsted for the Lord, and her throbbing thirst, never quenched, made her desire him all the more.

Experiencing Life's Sufferings in Company With Christ

My first priestly assignment was as associate pastor of Our Lady of Sorrows Parish in a northern suburb of Memphis. It is an assignment I remember with great fondness; the friendships I made there have endured, and I maintain contact with a number of parishioners. I have watched their kids grow up, accompanied them through tough times, celebrated their weddings, and baptized their children.

The Church celebrates the feast of the Exaltation of the Holy Cross on September 14 and the feast of Our Lady of Sorrows the following day. The bond between the cross of Christ and the love of his mother is very strong, and it is important as we reflect on — and experience — the cross in our lives that we see in Mary a compassionate, faithful model. Despite her fears, Mary allowed herself to be caught up trustingly in the mystery of her Son, and thus she shows us the way to peaceful surrender.

A passage in John Steinbeck's *The Grapes of Wrath* has always intrigued me. The novel chronicles the hardships of the members of the fictional Joad family, victims of the 1930s Oklahoma dust storms, who leave everything behind for the promised land of California. The heroine is Ma Joad, a weathered, gracious woman who has gained a kind of earthy wisdom through suffering. She had learned that in a mysterious way we can emerge from suffering not only in one piece but somehow even more whole than before.

She once tried, with great frustration, to explain this mystery to her daughter, Rose of Sharon:

"They's a time of change, an' when that comes, dyin' is a piece of all dyin', and bearin' is a piece of all bearin', and bearin' an' dyin' is two pieces of the same thing. An' then things ain't lonely any more. An' then a hurt don't hurt so bad, 'cause it ain't a lonely hurt no more, Rosasharn. I wisht I could tell you so you'd know, but I can't."

> *"At the cross her station keeping, stood the mournful mother weeping, close to Jesus to the last."*
> (Stabat Mater)

Have you ever tried to teach your children something which you know from the bottom of your heart is true — something you would stake your fortune on — but found that words cannot convey that truth? You know they have to experience it somehow, even with pain and struggle, before they know what you are talking about. It is a frightening prospect that they will have to learn through suffering, and you would prefer to spare them the pain by putting the lessons into simple, convincing words. You wish you could tell them so they'd know, but you can't.

It is difficult to send children into the world, knowing what they might face, because they are so precious to us. Seeing into their future is impossible, as is keeping them under our watchful eye forever. It is for that reason that parents spend so much time giving them a foundation of faith and morality, because only these give true insight into how to live. Even after the foundation is firm, however, there are uncertainties.

The sequence for September 15 is the *Stabat Mater*, which begins, "At the cross her station keeping, stood the mournful mother weeping, close to Jesus to the last." The mystery of the cross of Christ is deeply intertwined with the life of his mother, because from the moment of her conception she was destined to be joined to him in everything. When in his Gospel St. John shows Mary at the foot of the cross, she is there not only as his mother but also as our representative and mother. The mother of Jesus, who had once been told that her heart would be pierced by a sword, watched as he suffered and died. What must have been going through her head and her heart?

Ma Joad knew something of the secrets of life because of her experience, but Mary allowed herself to be taken much further, through faith, into the very mystery of her Son. She is the perfect patroness of mothers at every stage of their children's lives — from conception to the first day of school, from adolescence to moving out of the house, from marriage to their own family responsibilities.

Through Baptism, our entire lives are intertwined with the mystery of Christ, and mothers know the joy as well as the pain that can accompany their children's participation in that mystery, especially when it entails suffering. Mary is "Our Lady of Sorrows" because she trusted that through it all, the Father would bring victory to his precious Son, and that Jesus' suffering would bear fruit in his Father's plan. In one sense, she had to "let go" of her Son, but in another sense, she never did. She offered him back to his Father for the salvation of the world, but she clung to him with love as only a mother can. She followed him as a disciple to show us the way.

When we let go of our children into life, we are actually doing as Mary did — giving them over to the Father's care. Mothers can know instinctively, as Mary knew, that God's love for us must be truly unfathomable if he would give his Son for our sakes. It is that same mysterious Love who guards our children with all his might.

Aunt Merle's Lesson on Pain

My Aunt Merle knew about suffering. A pediatric nurse by training, she bravely endured the painful and disfiguring effects of rheumatoid arthritis for more than forty-five years, until her death in late 2009. In the midst of her battle with disease, she kept working because of her indomitable spirit, her love for nursing, and her realization that not working would be worse for her than continuing to work, despite the limitations her illness imposed upon her.

In many ways, Merle and her sisters were the hub of our large extended family. They made sure we were remembered on our birthdays and other special occasions, comforted in distress and counseled in confusion, and kept abreast of family news. Our lives were the center of their attention, and we nephews and nieces always knew we had a place in their hearts and at their supper table. Our clan grew because of them, for they welcomed into our family "adopted" nieces and nephews, about whom we heard so often that we thought of them as our own.

Merle had a particularly wry sense of humor, which we enjoyed immensely. She held strong opinions — and she had a heart of pure gold. Because of her heroic suffering, however, among the members of our family she also enjoyed deep respect. It wasn't just that she suffered bravely and perseveringly. She pondered, prayed, and grappled with God about her suffering, and she spent her life alleviating the suffering of children. In so doing, she gained immense wisdom. In her own inimitable way, with a hard-to-replicate slow, Southern drawl and typical droll directness, she dispensed that wisdom. We listened.

Just recently, one of my sisters told me of a conversation she had with Merle not long before she died. My sister had undergone painful surgery and was commiserating with Merle about its stubborn, lingering effects. She voiced embarrassment about mentioning pain to Merle, of all people. But Merle would have none of such embarrassment.

> *"I consider that the sufferings of this present time are as nothing compared with the glory to be revealed for us." (Romans 8:18)*

She said, "Listen, baby. Don't ever put yourself down for hurting. Your pain is your pain, and you feel it. Don't ever feel guilty about that. Just don't start thinking that your pain is the ONLY pain in the world."

My sister found comfort and assurance in that counsel, as we all should. None of us need go seeking pain and suffering. They are part and parcel of every human life and of the human condition itself. By the same token, none of us should deny the pain that comes our way. To do so could cause damaging physical, psychological, and spiritual effects; make us insensitive or intolerant of the suffering of others; and cause us to miss great lessons God wishes to teach us.

So clearly had God seen the suffering of his people that he sent his Son to reveal his limitless compassion and healing power. For it is not just we who needed God's healing, God's mercy, and God's salvation — creation itself needed to be taken to the cross and saved. According to St. Paul, creation groans in labor pains.

In *Romance* 7, "The Incarnation," sixteenth-century mystic St. John of the Cross poetically describes a conversation between God the Father and the Son, in which the Son expresses his desire to bring the Father's limitless love and healing power to us:

I will go and tell the world,
spreading the word
of your beauty and sweetness
and of your sovereignty.
I will go and seek my bride
and take upon myself
her weariness and labors
in which she suffers so;
and that she may have life
I will die for her
and lifting her out of that deep,
I will restore her to you.
(Romance 7, 9b–11)

No one knows our suffering as does the Lord, and he knows it from personal experience. He knows the pain that touches every sinew of the body, every crevice of the heart, every unbearable emotion, and every broken relationship. In his own agony and prayer to the Father about his suffering (the Gospel writers tell us he prayed Psalms 22 and 31 on the cross), he bore our agonies, every one. Discounting none of them, he embraced them; discounting none of us, he embraced us.

That is what Aunt Merle knew to the depths of her crippled, aching joints. Hers was not the only pain in the world, but it was real. In the unique way God called her to the cross, she learned many hard lessons and dispensed even more by her love. No doubt, because of her faith in the Lord Jesus, who knew suffering, she worked with him to restore many to God by her extraordinary example. She learned the profound and necessary lesson that her suffering was his, that his was hers.

Paul writes to the Romans,

> I consider that the sufferings of this present time are as nothing compared with the glory to be revealed for us.

> For creation awaits with eager expectation the revelation of the children of God; for creation was made subject to futility, not of its own accord but because of the one who subjected it, in hope that creation itself would be set free from slavery to corruption and share in the glorious freedom of the children of God. We know that all creation is groaning in labor pains even until now; and not only that, but we ourselves, who have the firstfruits of the Spirit, we also groan within ourselves as we wait for adoption, the redemption of our bodies. (Romans 8:18-23)

Yours is not the only pain in the world, nor is mine. When you suffer, go to Jesus. He has already been sent by the Father to meet you, for only he knows all the pain of the world.

CHAPTER 6
ALIVE FOR GOD IN CHRIST JESUS

The Wonder of Being Human

Whenever I hear the Scripture readings from the first three chapters of the Book of Genesis at Mass, I find it a good opportunity for reflection on the meaning of the beautiful accounts of creation.

After its depiction of each of the six days of creation, Genesis repeats a single refrain: "God saw that it was good." Light, the sky, the earth, the sea, vegetation, the sun, the moon, fish, birds, and animals of all kinds — creation unfolded in wondrous array, all of it good in God's eyes. But the climax of creation came when man and woman were created, for finally there was something in creation made "in the divine image." Having created man and woman, God handed dominion of the earth to them, and the refrain appears a seventh time: "God looked at everything he had made, and found it very good" (Genesis 1:31).

There could be no mistaking the important truth taught by Genesis: God made everything, including the crown of creation, man and woman. Wonderfully made in his image, our very being displays his wisdom. The unique dignity of the human person is spelled out in a number of ways in the Bible: Of all creation, only man and woman can know and love the creator; we alone are called to share, by knowledge and love, in God's own life. A human being is not just something; he or she is someone, a person. We are capable of self-knowledge and can give ourselves freely in love and communion with other persons.

We humans are also "body and soul." "Soul" refers to the innermost facet of our being, what is of most value in us, that by which we are most especially made in God's image, our spiritual principle. The human body also shares in the divine image; in fact, what makes our body "human" is precisely the fact that it is animated by a spiritual soul. The unity of body and soul in the human person forms a single nature, "human nature." The whole human person — body and soul — is saved by Christ and designed to become a temple of the Holy Spirit. The soul is immortal; it separates from the body at death, but the two are destined to be reunited at the final resurrection.

I have had the good fortune of seeing some of nature's most magnificent displays — the Grand Canyon, oceans, mountain ranges. I was awestruck by them all and often wished more friends and family were with me to share the experience.

What makes our body "human" is precisely the fact that it is animated by a spiritual soul.

Reflecting on the opening chapters of Genesis, however, I am reminded that as beautiful and awesome as the natural wonders of the world are, they pale in comparison to the crown of creation: the human person. We know we are created in God's image and likeness, but do we miss the full impact of that truth? In the midst of our daily routine — as we experience the world and its challenges, as we encounter the vulnerable and poor, and even as we choose entertainment — do we keep in mind the awesome image and likeness of God in one another? By comparison, the Grand Canyon is just another creek.

God's image and likeness give us a dignity that no other part of creation possesses, and the recognition of that dignity is the cornerstone of the Church's teaching about the sacredness of life. It calls us to examine the way we treat our family, our associates, and even those we have never met but see only on television. Sarcasm, selfishness, violence, injustice — these, too, are offenses against human dignity.

I have seen very little "reality TV." What I have seen has saddened me because it exploits people and their problems, making them objects of fascination, ridicule, scorn, and derision. Even if the characters willingly participate, we are still exploiting them. Such programs seductively and subtly erode our appreciation of human dignity. We cannot laugh at a real person's real misfortunes on television and then expect that we will not soon enough laugh at a coworker or neighbor.

Someday may we awaken to the abiding dignity of every human person, from the moment of conception to natural death, whether they are young or old, sick or poor, native or immigrant, innocent or guilty, educated or uneducated, victims of others' or their own mistakes, towers of strength or feet of clay, known or unknown to us.

We are the crown of creation. The gift of faith enables us to see creation as it truly is and challenges us to shape our behavior accordingly:

> When I see your heavens, the work of your fingers,
> the moon and stars that you set in place —
> What is man that you are mindful of him,
> and a son of man that you care for him?
> Yet you have made him little less than a god,
> crowned him with glory and honor. (Psalm 8:4-6)

St. Leo the Great wrote, "If we are indeed the temple of God and if the Spirit of God lives in us, then what every believer has within himself is greater than what he admires in the skies."

Our Freedom as Children of God

I have a close friend who was one of the thousands of soldiers to land on Omaha Beach in northern France on June 6, 1944 — D-Day. There's no question that D-Day played the pivotal role in victory for the Allies in World War II's European theater; it is a day often celebrated and memorialized for its acts of bravery and skill, a day so central to American history that a museum in New Orleans is dedicated entirely to its legacy.

I have known my friend well for more than twenty-five years, but rarely has he spoken about his experience that day. Once when we were driving back to my rectory after having seen the movie *Platoon*, I noticed that he was very quiet. As we pulled into the driveway, he made his only comment about the movie: "I had forgotten how terrible war is."

I heard my friend speak publicly about D-Day at a banquet during which he received an award. He spoke about the ironies of life, and about the fact that he has often asked himself why, among all his high school friends who were drafted into military service and among his many buddies in the Army, he was one of those who survived the war. He spoke about the enemy he faced, who in circumstances other than war could just as easily have been his friend. He spoke about the blessed freedom we enjoy as citizens of the United States and the responsibility that accompanies our freedom.

I did not meet him until he had already been a priest for twenty-two years. He had entered the seminary after the war and was ordained in December of 1952. I jokingly reminded him that I was only seven months old when he was ordained (he responded with a laugh, "Well, at least you were born!"). As part of my seminary training in the mid-1970s, I sometimes accompanied him to U.S. Army posts in northern Italy, where he served as a reserve chaplain while on the faculty of the North American College.

He fought for freedom in World War II, and in the intervening years he has been bringing the freedom of Christ to parishioners, seminarians, and priests. He is a meat-and-potatoes kind of priest (the "meat and potatoes" being prayer, the Eucharist, the Word of God, and love). I consider myself fortunate to have such a friend and mentor.

Each year as we celebrate Independence Day, I hope you enjoy the day as much as I do. For more than two hundred years, we citizens of the United States have prized our freedom, even though at times we have taken it for granted. Wartime has sometimes served to galvanize our patriotic spirit, as we realized what we were at risk of losing; sometimes prophetic voices have inspired us to expand our notion of the responsibilities that go hand in hand with American citizenship and have shown us the way to a different kind of patriotism, a different kind of freedom.

We have learned about freedom from slavery, and we are still learning about the importance of working for freedom from poverty, oppression, disease, racism, and addiction. We are experiencing a dramatic increase in immigration from other countries, particularly Mexico, as young men and families come here seeking a better life. Perhaps these freedoms are the great responsibility of our generation — helping others live fully human lives in peace and security.

As great as our American freedom is, it is only a shadow of the freedom we have as sons and daughters of God. Freedom is not the ability or the right to do as one pleases; one might choose to use drugs and end up "enslaved" to them. Do we call that freedom? Drug addiction offers a dramatic example of the dynamic that envelops us whenever we choose something that is not good for us, whenever we choose to do evil. Our destiny as human persons is to be with God forever, who is good itself. Evil is beneath our dignity. As long as I choose to do evil, I am not free.

Jesus' death and resurrection freed us from slavery to sin, regaining our eternal destiny with God that had been lost through sin. In other words, the freedom that comes from following the way of Jesus Christ is not just freedom "from" something; it is also freedom "for" something — freedom for communion with God. We make full use of that freedom only when we strive to do good. The power to determine what is good and what is evil is God's alone, so we look to him for the truth that sets us free. Following the way of Jesus is the way to freedom for humankind. The more we allow his way to be the guiding truth of our lives, the more we understand what true freedom is.

As great as our American freedom is, it is only a shadow of the freedom we have as sons and daughters of God.

We owe a debt of gratitude to those patriots who first won our freedom, to those who crafted our constitution, to those who fought in wars to preserve our freedom, to those who have taught us the responsibilities of freedom, and to our parents who reared us in freedom.

My priest friend who fought for freedom's sake on D-Day has helped me learn about the full measure of freedom that comes from faith in God and in his Son, who died that we might know the truth and be free for all eternity.

Building a World Sensitive to Human Dignity

Growing up in the '50s and '60s, I never liked to hear television programs broken up by that jarring announcement: "We interrupt this program to bring you a special news bulletin." Solemn and unadorned, those words never meant good news, and even as a kid I got a sinking feeling in my stomach. If breaking news occurred during school hours, our principal spoke unexpectedly over the loudspeaker.

One such announcement was made on April 4, 1968. Monsignor Paul Morris, principal of Bishop Byrne High School in Memphis, came over the loudspeaker to inform us that Dr. Martin Luther King Jr. had been murdered in our city. His statement was met with stunned silence and, no doubt, fear, as its meaning and its ramifications began to sink in. As I think back to that day, I wonder how the announcement sounded and what feelings it evoked for the few African-American students in our school, one of whom was among my closest friends. Did we go out of our way to show them comfort and kindness?

From an early age, I had been aware that our Southern city was divided by race and economics, though at first I did not fully understand how that division unjustly determined so many details of daily life. My parents had taught us to treat all people with respect, and they practiced what they preached.

The grocery and upscale department store in our neighborhood were like many others in the South of my youth. Among the characteristics they shared was a striking symbol: two drinking fountains, side by side, identical in every way, except that one bore a sign that read "White" and the other a sign that read "Colored." Even as a child, I was struck by the strangeness of that arrangement.

At the grocery store one day with our mother, one of my sisters and I became thirsty. We noticed that on the "Colored" fountain there was a small cup, and we held it under the stream of water. A man walked up and said, "You shouldn't drink from *that* cup." The incident made a lasting impression.

As I prepared for Confirmation in the sacristy of an Arkansas parish some years ago, I overheard a young boy ask the pastor if he needed servers. "Sure," said Father. "You can carry the cross."

The blond-headed boy quickly reappeared, vested in an alb and carrying the processional cross. A few moments later, he startled me with a question.

"Do you know what the KKK is?"

I was truly taken aback. "Yes," I said. "That's the Ku Klux Klan. We don't agree at all with what they stand for. Why are you asking about them?"

"I heard they're coming to town, and I'm afraid because my father and my sister are from Mexico." I tried to reassure him that his father and sister were in no danger, that the police would be aware of anything unusual that might be planned. Overhearing our conversation, his mother offered background on his question and added more reassuring words for her son. His sister, smiling, was talking with friends nearby. His father was in line for the entrance procession, for he would be a Confirmation sponsor. The entire family is bilingual.

It broke my heart that evening to confront the painful effects of racism again in such a powerful way. Anxiety was written on his face and in his question. With shame, I admit that my brief exchange with the server exposed to me once again my own lack of sensitivity to the insidious power of racism.

Reared in a home where racist attitudes were neither taught nor tolerated, I grew to understand more clearly why racism is sinful and antithetical to Christian faith. As a priest, I have preached about it.

But I have never had to face racist attitudes directed at me.

Sadly, racism is found even in parishes, a sign that we have not yet fully given ourselves in conversion to the Lord.

It took a server's anxious question to help me recognize at a more critical level how much work there is to be done — first and most foremost within myself, but also within our communities.

Hearing my young friend's question, I was awakened in a new way to what racism does to children, to struggling parents, to aging grandparents, to the courageous pioneers and modern-day workers in the civil rights movement — and to people like me, who aren't nearly as alert as we should be to its dangerous influence.

Needless to say, the South is by no means the exclusive domain of racism, for its roots and effects are found everywhere in the world. They take on local flavor and are often institutionalized according to hometown circumstances. Sadly, racism is found even in parishes, a sign that we have not yet fully given ourselves in conversion to the Lord.

As we mark Dr. King's birthday each year, my thoughts return to news bulletins, water coolers, his assassination in my hometown, and an anxious question posed by a twelve-year-old altar server.

Heavenly Father, teach us to build a world where little boys and girls, and their parents and grandparents, don't have to ask fearful questions. Help us rise above racism in all its forms that we may recognize and disarm its influence. May we never reject or frighten any of your little ones, for we are all your sons and daughters, made in your image. Amen.

Reading Life Through God's Lenses

It wasn't until I reached my forties that I began to notice how much fine print there is in life. Literally.

Nearsighted as I am, I resisted bifocals as long as I could, finding them awkward and dizzying. Particularly in the old days, when the only option available was a bifocal lens with annoying lines, I wasn't willing to make the effort. With a stubborn squint, I could read footnotes and label instructions, and that was good enough for me.

Years passed, my vision worsened, and I was no longer able to escape the inevitable. Fortunately for me, with graduated bifocal lenses the adjustment was not nearly as difficult as I had feared. I could read even the smallest print again — as long as I tilted my head at just the right angle.

More years passed, and I found myself whispering to altar servers holding the Missal to "back up," since it is easier to read words a few feet away than right in front of me. Now, if the server stands too close, I back up. Now, if I want to read the fine print, I take off my glasses.

As a child, I perceived that life was quite simple. Wake up, eat breakfast, go to school, come home, play with friends, eat supper, do homework, go to bed. There was fun in friendship and family, mysterious peacefulness at church, and lazy hours of freedom dreamed away with imagination. There were consequences to misbehavior, bad grades to reward laziness, and a neighborhood network of moms and dads to enforce commonly held rules.

In early adolescence, I noticed hints that life is not as carefree as I had thought. Rumors of nuclear bombs, and bomb shelters in the neighborhood, fascinated and frightened. The assassination of

President John F. Kennedy, reported by our principal on the loudspeaker, and later the assassinations of Dr. Martin Luther King Jr. and Robert F. Kennedy, were nightmares any way one looked at them. The war in Vietnam, the personal problems of friends and family, the struggle to grow up: Everything pointed to the inescapable conclusion that life is not always simple. There is fine print, hard to read and hard to decipher.

Part of maturing is learning the hard lesson that the fine print — unexpected, undeserved trials, the stuff no one could warn us about — is part of life.

Life is rarely simple. Sadly, for a variety of reasons some children never have the opportunity to experience a carefree childhood. Sooner or later, all of us face complicated problems requiring complicated solutions. Life can become so complex, our worlds turned so utterly upside down, that we wonder if the simple lessons we learned as children suffice for the real world. The fine print can be so overwhelming that in disappointment and desperation some folks reject those lessons completely. Why did they (why did God?) dupe me into believing back then that life is simple?

Part of maturing is learning the hard lesson that the fine print — unexpected, undeserved trials, the stuff no one could warn us about — is part of life. We move from the nearsightedness of youth, in which the world is made up of my house and neighborhood, to a farsighted capacity to see everything, the good and the bad. As little by little we understand hazards and complications, as we gradually recognize through friendship that we are not alone on the rough road, and as we are steadily stretched beyond ourselves in compassion for others, we are less startled by the fine print (even if no less infuriated or saddened by it at times). We might wish things could be simple as they were before, but in our heart of hearts we know that will not happen.

But are the simple lessons of childhood — the simple lessons of faith — inadequate for an adult life?

The Bible I use most often has tiny footnotes and cross-references I cannot read without taking off my bifocals. They give background information and explanations of difficult texts, but they don't change the message. They don't give complicated answers to complicated problems. Instead, they reinforce God's simple, timeless message to a people all too familiar with disappointment, failure, unexpected tragedy, and unspeakable suffering. The fine print in the Bible reads the same as the large print:

> I created you to share my life. Never forget I love you. I love you so much that when you ran away I sent my Son to bring you back. There is no reason to be afraid. Love others. Love yourself. Ask one another's forgiveness. Confess your sins and accept my forgiveness. Trust me. Be patient. Be generous. Be kind. Be peacemakers. Be thankful. Resist the devil and he will take flight. Pray without ceasing. Take up your cross and follow me. Take and eat my body broken for you, drink my blood poured out for you. I will never abandon you. Read further, and read again.

Indeed the fine print in the Bible reads the same as the large print, no matter what situation we find ourselves facing. To say that God's lessons are simple, however, is not to imply that they are naive, that they don't connect with the real world. Who better than Jesus understands the burdens of this world? The key to maturing as his disciple is to trust that his are the most important lessons to know by heart, the most important lenses we will ever need to see our way through the labyrinth of life.

Instruments of God's Goodness

Several years ago as I prepared to leave Little Rock for the Diocese of Joliet, the weeks were full of "farewells." I discovered that my emotions were on overdrive. Folks had been so good to me in Arkansas that I had many reasons to be grateful. Signs abounded that God's love was at work there. I also discovered that the best way to say good-bye is to give thanks, over and over. Conscious and careful thanksgiving is a powerful way to see God's footprints throughout one's life. That lesson was driven home for me one spring day before I left for Joliet, as I visited Memphis for the funeral of a priest friend.

I did not go to the cemetery immediately after the funeral Mass, planning to go later so that I could have some quiet time by myself. Mid-afternoon the sun was shining and a strong breeze was blowing across the eighty beautiful acres that comprise historic Calvary Cemetery in Memphis. Everything was in bloom, and it was a glorious day to be there.

My first stop was at the graves of my parents. Knowing that after moving north my opportunities to visit would be less frequent, I wanted to spend a few moments there. It was the perfect place to think and pray. I thanked them for all they did for me: rearing me, loving me, guiding me, sacrificing for me, forgiving me, and supporting me. I'm sure I don't know the half of it. I also asked them to pray for me, as I do every day, that I will be a good bishop and generous in God's service. I truly feel their prayers.

Next I visited the graves of some elderly friends I knew many years ago in my first parish assignment. Before his death, I had made a promise to Mike that I would visit his and Marie's graves each time I stopped by my parents' graves. Back to that in a moment.

Next I drove to the section of the cemetery called the "Priests' Mound," a hill topped with a marble altar and crucifix surrounded by the graves of priests who served in West Tennessee. I began at the most recent grave and stopped at each one, circling around the altar until I reached the graves of those who had died long before my time. At each marker, I remembered something about the priest and asked him to pray for me.

Please don't think I was sad that afternoon, or that spending so much time at the cemetery was a morbid farewell. To the contrary, I was at peace, realizing stop after stop that I have been blessed by good parents, good priest mentors, good friends, and good example from saintly parishioners. In so many words, God said to me, "See how good I've been to you?"

I was at peace, realizing stop after stop that I have been blessed by good parents, good priest mentors, good friends, and good example from saintly parishioners.

Back to the elderly former parishioners whose graves I always visit: I once wrote a column about them, explaining that in the late 1970s I visited their home monthly on my First Friday Communion call route. I have always recalled those visits as full of sweetness and faith. I can picture the two of them in their simple home, deeply in love with each other and with the Lord, as if it were yesterday.

Do you know what I discovered a few years after writing that column? I never met Marie! She died before I was assigned to the parish. At first, I was taken aback by that discovery and thought there must be some mistake on the grave marker. I remembered her as clear as a bell. I could picture her sitting in their living room. But there was no mistake. I had never met her.

Not long afterward, I told my secretary about this strange experience. She commented, "Isn't it wonderful that Mike's love for her was so strong that even though you never met her, his telling you about her was filled with such tender detail that he painted a beautiful portrait of her in your mind?" That's exactly what had happened. His grateful love had etched a lasting image of her in my memory.

That's why it's crucial that we give thanks in loving detail for God's blessings and the people who have crossed our paths. Not only are we giving God his due for all he's done for us — we're also painting portraits of his goodness in our memories, portraits that stay with us throughout life as never-failing evidence of his abounding presence.

"The Name of That Boat Was Love"

I have often thought about the irony that as I was writing a series of columns in Arkansas about Catholic teaching on health and end-of-life decisions, my mother experienced a serious downturn in health, which led to her death on September 7, 2005. Some years earlier, she had granted me durable power of attorney for health care (sometimes called "health care proxy"). She went this route rather than complete an "advance medical directive" (sometimes called a "living will"), preferring not to check a list of options that may be difficult to interpret in the concrete. We talked about her wishes, and she summarized by saying simply, "If you have to make decisions about my health care, I just want to make sure they are in keeping with Church teaching."

That's the way Mom was. Independent by nature, having raised five kids and widowed at fifty-one, she was quite capable of taking good care of herself until several years before her death. Independent as she was, the guide she always clung to trustingly was her Catholic faith and its teachings.

In early 2005, it became clear to my sisters and me that it was time for Mom to leave her home of forty-seven years and move to a place where she could remain independent but safe and receive the care she needed. It was a tough decision, a painful "letting-go," but Mom took it in stride.

After making the move to a Catholic assisted-living facility, she began to realize it had been the right thing, but still she grieved the loss of her house and the self-emptying this new stage of life required of her. The day she visited the empty house to say good-bye and inspect the moving project my family had undertaken on her behalf, she told one of my sisters, "There was a lot of good living in this house."

As the months passed, her health declined and she slowed considerably; her memory began to fail, her heart ailments worsened, and other complications arose. When I visited her on August 30, she told me she thought the Lord was going to call her soon. The next morning she was taken by ambulance to the hospital, where she spent the last week of her life in the intensive-care unit.

It was a true blessing that all five of us kids were able to spend most of that week with her and with one another. We prayed with and for her, talked to her, told family stories, and tried to do what we could to make her comfortable when she was restless or in pain. Two of my sisters sang quietly to her. Many relatives and friends visited.

In the early days, she was conscious part of the time and spoke about dying, but as the week wore on she mostly slept, though often fitfully. Late in the afternoon of September 7, one of my nieces noticed that her heart rate began to slow, and within twenty minutes she died.

We knew the day she entered the hospital that decisions would have to be made about her medical care, and although I had durable power of attorney for health care, I wanted every member of the family to be involved in those decisions. I asked a physician who is a family friend to meet with us to answer questions about her condition, prognosis, and care. The meeting was extremely helpful and allowed us to air our thoughts and feelings and remind one another of what Mom had said about her wishes. With the doctor's help, we prayerfully reached consensus about Mom's care. It was a comfort to see how Church teaching gave us good direction and peace of mind.

As difficult as it was to see Mom suffer physically the last two years of her life, it was inspiring to watch as she struggled to understand how God was at work in her suffering and dying. We could love and comfort her, but this journey was hers to make. As we kept vigil that final week, it became clear that something truly holy and mysterious was taking place: the ultimate "letting-go" on Mom's part, the ultimate "calling" on God's part. As she had done in life, she now gave herself to God in the mystery of dying, trusting that though it was not easy, God would see her through.

We wondered out loud what she was thinking and seeing and asked God to help us understand how he was at work. A thousand thoughts and feelings, a thousand memories, and a thousand quiet moments passed through the darkened room. We realized that as Mom was close to God in death, we were close to him at her bedside.

We realized that as Mom was close to God in death, we were close to him at her bedside.

Someone recently gave me a holy card with these beautiful words of St. John of the Cross:

> And I saw the river over which every soul must pass to reach the kingdom of heaven. And the name of that river was Suffering.... And I saw the boat which carried souls across the river. And the name of that boat was Love.

It helps me to write about Mom's final days, and I hope it helps you to know that Catholic teaching about the end of life is an expression of God's love for the lives he has created and redeemed. Jesus experienced human suffering and death, and in Baptism we were joined to his victory over them. Our suffering and our death, as mysterious and painful as they might be, find their meaning in him who died for us and draws us to himself. No one who places trust in him in living or in dying will ever be disappointed.

Lifted High, Pulled Deep Into His Heart

On somber November days, as we look out our windows and walk the streets, watching leaves fall against the backdrop of a wet, gray sky, the Church reminds us that as Christians we are full of hope. Why, during what might seem a season of gloom, are we full of hope? Because we are never alone.

Gloomy weather can affect our mood — and a gloomy heart can affect the way we view the weather! If one is prone to feelings of loneliness, a gray sky can amplify the sense of being alone. If one is grieving the loss of a loved one, no matter how long ago he or she died, a dreary sky can weigh down the heart and rob precious memories of their ability to bring us joy.

But the Church proclaims to us from the very first day of November:

> [T]oday by your gift we celebrate the festival
> of your city,
> the heavenly Jerusalem, our mother,
> where the great array of our brothers and sisters
> already gives you eternal praise.
>
> Towards her, we eagerly hasten, as pilgrims advancing
> by faith,
> rejoicing in the glory bestowed upon those
> exalted members of the Church
> through whom you give us, in our frailty, both strength
> and good example. (Preface of All Saints)

In the Church, we are always surrounded with the saints and angels, who cheer us on our journey to God, give us inspirational example, and pray for us.

In *Prayer in Practice*, Dominican Father Simon Tugwell writes:

> From this valley of tears, we can already begin to live off the wealth of heaven; we are surrounded and supported by a great cloud of witnesses, and so can undertake to run our course with endurance and without losing heart. And even if we do lose heart, they do not lose heart, even if we are overcome by terror, they are not overcome by terror, even if we are broken by grief they are not broken by grief; … we are one with them in Christ, members of one another.

Because the saints see God in his fullness, they know there is no reason to fear. They see directly; we see with the eyes of faith. Though our emotions and the trials of life sometimes make us uneasy or doubtful, it is not the same with them. They hold us up when we falter, lift us up in prayer when we run out of words.

As we think about and pray for our deceased loved ones, we recognize that they are safely in God's loving hands.

November is also the month when we remember our beloved dead. The Church, even as she proclaims the joy and hope of the Resurrection, knows how to grieve and gives us comfort in our celebration of All Souls' Day. Who could not grieve the loss of those we love? When the love is deep, so is the grief. As we think about and pray for our deceased loved ones, we recognize that they are safely in God's loving hands.

Our loved ones who, by God's loving providence, are experiencing purification to prepare them to see him face-to-face, also pray for us! They know they are on their way to heaven, and by whatever means God chooses to prepare them, they are filled with hope. So would they want us to be filled with hope as well. Pope Benedict XVI, addressing the clergy of Rome in 2008, said:

> Purgatory basically means that God can put the pieces back together again. That he can cleanse us in such a way that we are able to be with him and can stand there in the fullness of life. Purgatory strips off from one person what is unbearable and from another the inability to bear certain things, so that in each of them a pure heart is revealed, and we can see that we all belong together in one enormous symphony of being.

Our grieving hearts say to us of our loved ones who have died, "We belong together!" And God says to us in response, "You're right! You have all been made to be together forever in me. My grace is at work in this temporary separation, in this great, mysterious 'symphony of being.' Be at peace and know that your loved ones are safely, hopefully, with me."

In his encyclical *Saved in Hope*, Pope Benedict reminds us that prayer is the path of communion with God when we feel alone:

> A first essential setting for learning hope is prayer. When no one listens to me anymore, God still listens to me. When I can no longer talk to anyone or call upon anyone, I can always talk to God. When there is no longer anyone to help me deal with a need or expectation that goes beyond the human capacity for hope, he can help me. When I have been plunged into complete solitude ... if I pray I am never totally alone.

We were made to be together; we were made for communion; we were made for love. With every step we take, the Good

Shepherd is gathering us in the Church and preparing us for that final, perfect communion. In other words, through the Church we are already "in this together." Our seeming separation from loved ones is only temporary, and the final communion for which we are destined will be something beyond words, beyond our capacity to imagine. We and they will all be there together — in God — and every hope will be fulfilled.

Gray skies can draw us into deep, quiet, and grateful reflection on our blessings, the loved ones who have passed through our lives and surround us still, and the God who is closer to us than we are to ourselves — the God who is always waiting with an outstretched hand to both lift us high and pull us deep into his heart, his loving embrace.

CHAPTER 7

GOD'S SURPRISE CHOICE: A WITNESS FOR OUR TIME

St. John Paul II: We Were Drawn to Christ by Christ

I would like to end this collection of columns with a tribute to St. John Paul II. All of us have heroes and heroines, and he tops my list. He remains an inspiration to millions around the world, a sign of Christian hope and an indefatigable witness to Jesus Christ.

In the fall of 1978, I was a newly ordained priest, having just returned to Rome for a final year of studies. That summer had been a historic one, with the death of Pope Paul VI in early August and the historically brief thirty-day reign of Pope John Paul I. After a summer of ministry at home, I arrived back in Rome in early October, just in time for the conclave that would elect a new pope.

Late each afternoon we students would go to St. Peter's Square along with thousands of others, anticipating that one day soon we would see white smoke billowing from the flue atop the

Sistine Chapel. The afternoon of October 16, our expectations were fulfilled. Black smoke turned to gray and then to white, preparing us for the announcement that a new pope had been elected.

A few hours passed before the announcement was made, and when one of the cardinals appeared at a balcony of St. Peter's to announce the news, an unfamiliar name was pronounced — Wojtyła. Many of us scoured the recent edition of the Vatican newspaper, which had published photographs of all the cardinals. Most of us would not have guessed that a name pronounced "voy-tee-wa" would begin with "W," and it took time to find the right photo. Among the Polish people present in St. Peter's Square that night, however, there was no doubt who had been elected pope — their beloved native son. They already knew the gift the Church universal was receiving, and that gift would unfold for the rest of us over the next twenty-six years.

In the early 1920s, the cobbled streets of Wadowice echoed with the soft young voice of a mother calling her son: "Karol … Karol … Karol …" It was time to come home, time to come inside, time to go to bed, time for prayers. How Karol cherished the way she called him, the family that embraced him, and the father and brother who made his family complete. He would hear his mother's sweet voice calling his name only until he was nine years old, the year of her death.

Later he would remember in poetry his own voice responding to hers on those Wadowice streets:

My place flows by in memory. The silence
of those distant streets does not pass away,
held up in space like glass which limpid eyes
break into sapphire and light. Nearest
are the child's words on which silence takes wing:
Mamma — Mamma —
then silence falls again into the same streets,

an invisible bird.
There I have returned many a time to memories....
("First Moment of the Glorified Body")

It would be only three years later that he would lose his brother, eleven years later that he would lose his father, and then be alone. It is said that he knelt twelve hours in prayer the night his father died.

Karol Józef Wojtyła was planted firmly in the earth, in a country, in an age, and in a beloved family. The circumstances of his life determined, by the grace of God, who he was and who he was to be. He never forgot who had given him birth or who had stood shoulder-to-shoulder with him as fellow countrymen and women. More significantly, he never forgot that it was God who strengthened him in difficulty, God who showed him the "why" of his life, God who brought his life to flower. Faith had taken root in Karol at a young age, just as he had taken root in Poland. The two were inseparably joined in him, and both made him strong.

By grace he heard God's call to be a priest, to love with all his heart the family God entrusted to him.

Karol was a man of the twentieth century. Formed by the personal circumstances of his family, as others of his time had been formed, he knew poverty and loss. Molded by political forces beyond his control, gathered into a brotherhood longing for freedom, he knew oppression and tyranny. Sculpted by steadfast Catholic faith, and gifted with ears and eyes and heart for the things of God, he listened hopefully and confidently for a word from God. He rested peacefully in the compassionate heart of the Mother of God and put everything in her hands at the foot of the cross.

At an early age, God had planted in him the capacity to read the signs of the times, to suffer the aches of his sisters and brothers. He longed — intensely — for something better; he hoped — fiercely — that God would have his way; he loved — deeply — whoever had want; he believed — bravely — in a time and place where faith was not allowed. He grew strong and graceful as an eagle.

By grace he heard God's call to be a priest, to love with all his heart the family God entrusted to him. Love them he did, calling their names in the streets of Kraków, listening as they called his in return. "Uncle" they nicknamed him at his suggestion, and he smiled to think they were responding to God's love.

Reflecting on his ordination to the priesthood in the book *Gift and Mystery*, St. John Paul wrote,

> The one about to receive Holy Orders prostrates himself completely and rests his forehead on the church floor, indicating in this way his complete willingness to undertake the ministry being entrusted to him.

At the Second Vatican Council, he looked down at the marble floor of St. Peter's Basilica and remembered how he had lain prostrate on just such a floor at his ordination to the priesthood, a humble sign of his complete willingness to undertake the ministry. Again he expressed himself in poetry:

> Peter, you are the floor, that others
> may walk over you … not knowing
> where they go. You guide their steps …
> You want to serve their feet that pass
> as rock serves the hooves of sheep.
> The rock is a gigantic temple floor,
> the cross a pasture.
> ("Marble Floor," 1962)

As he wrote those words, he did not know that sixteen years later he would take the place of Peter and become a rock for the sheep he was to feed and tend at the Lord's behest. He explains the poem in *Gift and Mystery*:

> In lying prostrate on the floor in the form of a cross before one's ordination, in accepting in one's life — like Peter — the cross of Christ and becoming with the Apostle a "floor" for our brothers and sisters, one finds the ultimate meaning of all priestly spirituality.

I was blessed to see St. John Paul II many times, several of those times literally "up close and personal." I would like to share two particular memories with you.

It was his custom to allow priests to concelebrate his private morning Mass in the chapel of his residence at the Vatican. I had the great blessing of doing so at least three times. Each time, those of us concelebrating would be ushered quietly into the chapel to find him kneeling (or in his later years, sitting) before the tabernacle, praying. The chapel was absolutely silent except for one sound: the sound of the pope's groaning. I have no doubt he was completely unaware of this — but as he prayed, from some place deep within his heart, he groaned. That sound is indelibly etched in my own heart, as I remember St. Paul's comments that we and all creation groan as we await "adoption, the redemption of our bodies," and how the Holy Spirit "comes to the aid of our weakness ... and intercedes with inexpressible groanings" (see Romans 8:18-27).

The second memory is of an incident in 2004, when I was in Rome for our *ad limina* visit, a visit every bishop in the world makes to the pope every five years. Part of the visit is a private audience with the pope.

What does one say to the pope? I was fortunate to be with him on May 18, his eighty-fourth birthday. His health was failing and he showed clear signs of Parkinson's disease, but his mind — and sense of humor — were very much intact. I began by wishing him a happy birthday and told him a bit about Arkansas, where I was serving at the time. However, I couldn't help but mention October 16, 1978.

"Holy Father, I had the privilege of being in the square the evening you were elected."

"Five o'clock," he said, smiling warmly.

"I will always remember that evening," I told him.

"I will remember, too," he responded with another smile.

What struck me about that exchange — the small talk that gushed from my lips, his smile and frailty — was simply that he warmly and paternally received *me*. That brief encounter moved me deeply because I knew I was in the presence of a pastor, *the* Pastor.

I often had that sense when reading his homilies and encyclicals. *Novo Millennio Ineunte*, for example, is clearly the work of a pastor. The Holy Father's reflections on the diverse groups of pilgrims particularly caught my eye:

> I have been impressed this year by the crowds of people which have filled St. Peter's Square at the many celebrations. I have often stopped to look at the long queues of pilgrims waiting patiently to go through the Holy Door. In each of them I tried to imagine the story of a life, made up of joys, worries, sufferings; the story of someone whom Christ had met and who, in dialogue with him, was setting out again on a journey of hope.

Those are the words of a pastor who saw with his heart, who desired to know the individuals in a crowd, and who embraced all.

The cobbled streets of Wadowice and Kraków had once been filled with the echoes of his conversation and his prayer, but after 1978 the streets of all the earth would be paved with his Peter-like strength — the cross of Christ on his shoulders so that we could walk sure-footed in hope. The years of his pontificate were filled with clear words of Catholic teaching, courageous solidarity with the oppressed and poor, a common touch that touched us all, a youthful smile that inspired the young to follow Jesus, a hope that cancels fear.

The years of his pontificate were filled with clear words of Catholic teaching, courageous solidarity with the oppressed and poor, a common touch that touched us all.

At the time of his funeral, and in the weeks surrounding his beatification, we marveled at the pictures of those Roman streets swelling beyond capacity with the family that came to bid him farewell and celebrate his beatification. We noticed how they all — how we all — thought of him as uncle, as father. We saw the leaders of religions and nations who came to honor him. But did we realize that it was not just him we loved but most especially Christ in him? It was Christ who brought him to flower.

Less than a year before his death, he wrote, in his book *Rise, Let Us Be On Our Way*:

> The Bishop is the sign of Christ's presence in the world, going out to meet men and women where they are: calling them by name, helping them to rise, consoling them with the Good News and gathering them into one around the Lord's Table.... He becomes for these people a sign that their isolation is ended, because he brings them into fellowship with Christ.

It is clear to me that the worldwide family members of Pope John Paul II who packed the streets of Rome in 2005 and again in 2011 were drawn by Christ, whether they realized it or not. These millions were drawn by Christ, to Christ in St. John Paul II.

How many times in his twenty-six years as pope did we hear him say the words of the risen Christ, "Peace be with you" — "Do not be afraid"? So convinced was he that in Christ we have everything that he proclaimed him in season and out of season.

This man of the twentieth century allowed himself to be so completely transformed by the Gospel that in him we saw the face of Christ. Billions throughout the world responded in respect, love, and faith. But make no mistake — even if they did not realize it, they were being drawn to Christ. That says something extremely important to you and me about the richness of our Catholic faith and about what Christ wants to do in and through us.

On the evening of Saturday, April 2, 2005, a different voice called out a familiar name. "Karol … Karol … Karol," said the archbishop after John Paul II died. But he received no response, so the announcement was made to the world that Karol had returned to the home of his Father. His voice still echoes through the streets of Rome, Wadowice, Kraków, Gdańsk, Nowa Huta, Mexico City, New York, Nairobi, Toronto, Paris, Denver, Jerusalem, and a host of places around the world, calling us by name, reminding us that we are not alone, and bidding us to come home. The songs sung in those very streets, paved in stone and marble and the rock that is Peter, blend into one chorus of praise to Christ, the Redeemer of the world, who made Karol Józef Wojtyła who he was.

"I am about to lay aside this book, and you are soon going away, each to his own business. It has been good for us to share the common light, good to have enjoyed ourselves, good to have been glad together. When we part from one another, let us not depart from him."

— FROM A TREATISE ON JOHN BY ST. AUGUSTINE
(LITURGY OF THE HOURS)